DRESSINGS

DRESSINGS

MAMIE FENNIMORE

CIDER MILL PRESS

BOOK PUBLISHERS

Dressings

13-Digit ISBN: 9781604337181

10-Digit ISBN: 1604337184

This book may be ordered by mail from the publisher. Please include $5.99 for postage and handling. Please support your local bookseller first!

Books published by Cider Mill Press Book Publishers are available at special discounts for bulk purchases in the United States by corporations, institutions, and other organizations. For more information, please contact the publisher.

Cider Mill Press Book Publishers
"Where good books are ready for press"
501 Nelson Place
Nashville, Tennessee 37214
cidermillpress.com

Typography: Bushcraft, Helvetica Rounded, and Sentinel

Image Credits: All images used under official license from Shutterstock.com.

Printed in Malaysia

24 25 26 27 COS 11 10 9 8

For my family, to whom I owe everything.

Contents

Introduction

Ideally, a dressing requires no more than four ingredients and five minutes to prepare. And yet too often we forgo that extra step when making a dish. It's understandable, of course; who wants one more thing to plan around? And is the storebought stuff really so bad? Of course not! But this book asks you to think about it differently: How much better can your meal be if you take that extra few minutes?

Think for a second about the side salad you serve at dinner. Sometimes you take the time to make a beautiful, elaborate dish; sometimes you empty the pre-packaged salad contents into a bowl and call it a day. But whether you're eating a salad that deserves a complex, balanced dressing to match, or elevating a simple salad into something special, homemade dressing will help. Even the most basic vinaigrette will impress your audience, no matter how particular their taste buds are.

This book may be small, but don't let its size fool you. Inside you'll find dressings, sauces and marinades for any dish—recipes versatile enough to allow you to mix, match, substitute or remove ingredients, all while creating a unique eating experience for even the most salad-averse eater. The simple foundations laid out in this little book allow you to build hundreds of deliciously simple and sometimes unconventional recipes that dress anything.

Just as you sourced your greens, veggies, and other salad ingredients with care, choose the building blocks of your dressings the same way. Don't shroud those gorgeous greens you so carefully picked out from the farmers market with something everybody's had before. And even if you're just cooking for one, the fun of a homemade dressing is that you rarely feel bored with a dressing's flavor profile—when you do, that just opens up the door for experimentation.

This is your dressing bible; with its help, you'll celebrate fresh produce with dressings that elevate and enhance the natural flavors on your table. I promise, your meals will never taste the same.

Vinaigrettes

Acidic, bright, aromatic—the vinaigrette is a basic essential to any home cook. Great for entertaining, casual dining or day-to-day life, homemade vinaigrettes are an easy and fun way to impress not only your guests but also yourself! Experimentation is the key to this section; the classic vinaigrette is a simple framework, upon which you can base endless variations. Be prepared to mix and match your favorite oils and vinegars, and to find your signature vinaigrette. I love trying new combinations to better understand how flavors complement one another on the palate. Use these to brighten up greens, vegetables or any meat or fish that needs a marinade.

Classic Balsamic Vinaigrette

ACTIVE TIME: 5 MINUTES • **TOTAL TIME: 5 MINUTES** • **SERVING SIZE: ¾ CUP**

A must-know for any salad lover, this simple recipe will serve you well forever!

Shake all ingredients in a jar and serve.

INGREDIENTS:

3 tablespoons balsamic vinegar

½ cup extra virgin olive oil

½ teaspoon sea salt

½ teaspoon black pepper, freshly ground

TIP: DRIZZLE YOUR DRESSING DOWN THE SIDES OF AN EMPTY BOWL AND THEN TOSS THE LETTUCE IN THE "DRESSED" BOWL. THE LEAVES WILL COAT MORE EVENLY AND WITHOUT ANY EXTRA BRUISING. PLUS YOU CAN ALWAYS ADD MORE DRESSING AS NEEDED.

Flavored Balsamic Vinegars

ACTIVE TIME: 20 MINUTES • TOTAL TIME: 20 MINUTES • SERVING SIZE: ¾ CUP

This basic template for flavored balsamic vinegar allows you to get creative. Check out the sidebar for strawberry alternatives, or try your own spin! If you want to make a fruit-flavored vinegar without the balsamic flavor, just substitute white wine vinegar for the balsamic. I recommend making this recipe a day before using the finished project; the longer you let your concoction steep, the more intense the flavor will be.

INGREDIENTS:

¾ cup balsamic vinegar

2 cups fresh strawberries

1 teaspoon honey

¼ teaspoon salt

1 In a small saucepan, bring the balsamic vinegar to a simmer and let it reduce to approximately / cup.

2 Add the diced strawberries, salt and honey and bring to boil.

3 Reduce heat to low and let simmer for 6 minutes, or until strawberries are softened. Crush the strawberries with spoon and let simmer for 10 more minutes or until mixture resembles a syrup. Remove from heat and let cool.

4 Let your flavored balsamic steep for a long time—preferably 12 hours. Strain out the pulp before serving for better consistency.

TRY INFUSING WITH ANY OF THESE FLAVORS INSTEAD!

- 2 CUPS RASPBERRIES
- 2 CUPS BLACKBERRIES
- 2 CUPS BLUEBERRIES
- 2 CUPS CRANBERRIES
- 2 CUPS FIGS
- 2 CUPS CHERRIES
- 2 CUPS POMEGRANATE
- 2 CUPS RHUBARB
- 10 SPRIGS OF THYME
- 5 SPRIGS OF ROSEMARY
- 3 SPRIGS OF OREGANO OR 2 TEASPOONS DRIED OREGANO
- 1 TEASPOON ESPRESSO POWDER OR 2 TABLESPOONS OF CRUSHED ESPRESSO BEANS

White Balsamic Vinaigrette

Local honey is a miracle in a jar. Since the bees are from your surrounding area, the pollen they use to make honey contains the very allergens that bother you each season. By eating local honey you build up your immune system!

INGREDIENTS:

3 tablespoons white balsamic vinegar

½ cup extra virgin olive oil

1 teaspoon Dijon mustard

½ teaspoon sea salt

½ teaspoon black pepper, freshly ground

1 teaspoon local honey

Whisk everything except the oil in a medium bowl. As you whisk, slowly drizzle in olive oil to emulsify your dressing.

> **IF YOU'RE PRESSED FOR TIME, SIMPLY SHAKE ALL INGREDIENTS IN A JAR AND SERVE.**

Gale's Glaze

The Dijon mustard really makes this recipe special; it acts as an emulsifier for the oil and vinegar, making your dressing thick and glossy. This glaze is perfect for a simple mixed green salad or grilled chicken.

Whisk all ingredients in a small bowl until mixture has emulsified.

INGREDIENTS:

3 tablespoons balsamic vinegar

½ cup extra virgin olive oil

1 teaspoon sea salt

1 teaspoon honey

1 teaspoon Dijon mustard

½ teaspoon black pepper, freshly ground

Red Wine Vinaigrette

ACTIVE TIME: 5 MINUTES • TOTAL TIME: 5 MINUTES • SERVING SIZE: ¾ CUP

This recipe is so simple and really comes in handy in a pinch. Use it to elevate your lunchtime salad!

INGREDIENTS:

3 tablespoons red wine vinegar

½ cup extra virgin olive oil

1 teaspoon Dijon mustard

1 shallot, minced

½ teaspoon sea salt

½ teaspoon black pepper, freshly ground

Whisk ingredients in a small bowl or shake them in a jar and serve.

White Wine Vinaigrette

If you want to make a wine vinaigrette with a bit more tang, try this equally easy recipe on for size.

Whisk ingredients in a small bowl or shake them in a jar and serve.

INGREDIENTS:

2 tablespoons white wine vinegar

1 tablespoon lemon juice, freshly squeezed

1 teaspoon lemon zest

½ cup extra virgin olive oil

½ teaspoon sea salt

½ teaspoon black pepper, freshly ground

Champagne Vinaigrette

Champagne vinegar is great for a more delicate salad that requires a lighter-bodied dressing. This vinaigrette is fruity and clean and will toss beautifully with your greens.

Whisk ingredients in a small bowl or shake them in a jar and serve.

INGREDIENTS:

3 tablespoons champagne vinegar

½ cup extra virgin olive oil

½ teaspoon sea salt

½ teaspoon black pepper, freshly ground

1 teaspoon honey

Sherry Wine Vinaigrette

ACTIVE TIME: 5 MINUTES • TOTAL TIME: 5 MINUTES • SERVING SIZE: ¾ CUP

Classically a Spanish condiment, sherry vinegar is a great way to shake up a basic vinaigrette's flavor. Now that this kind of vinegar is more widely available, we can use it more often and not limit it to Spanish dishes. Sherry has the complex, savory notes of oak and toasted nuts, setting this vinegar apart from others on the shelf.

INGREDIENTS:

3 tablespoons sherry vinegar

½ cup olive oil

½ teaspoon salt

½ teaspoon black pepper, freshly ground

½ teaspoon granulated sugar

Whisk ingredients in a small bowl or shake them in a jar and serve.

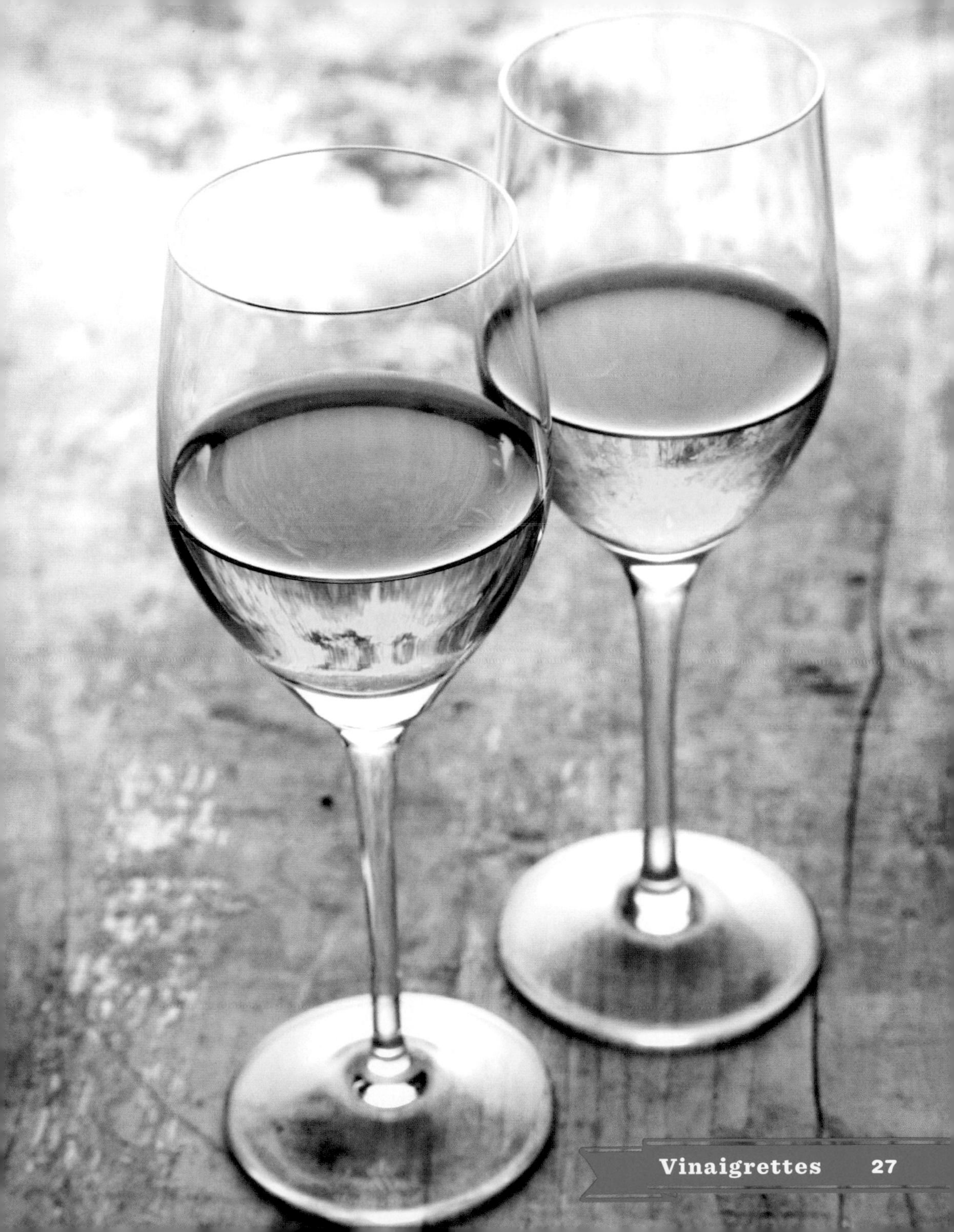

Apple Cider Vinaigrette

ACTIVE TIME: 5 MINUTES • TOTAL TIME: 5 MINUTES • SERVING SIZE: ¾ CUP

This is one of my favorites in the book. Although this is a year-round vinaigrette, autumn salads absolutely crave this sweet and tangy vinegar. Drizzle this appley gold over kale, walnuts and craisins and serve alongside your favorite fall meal.

Whisk ingredients in a small bowl or shake them in a jar and serve.

INGREDIENTS:

3 tablespoons apple cider vinegar

½ cup olive oil or grape seed oil

½ teaspoon sea salt

½ teaspoon black pepper, freshly ground

1 teaspoon honey

Rice Wine Vinaigrette

When looking for a light vinaigrette that won't overwhelm your taste buds, choose rice wine vinegar. It is perfect for any Asian-inspired salad.

Whisk ingredients in a small bowl or shake them in a jar and serve.

INGREDIENTS:

3 tablespoons rice wine vinegar

½ cup vegetable or grape seed oil

1 teaspoon salt

1 teaspoon black pepper, freshly ground

1 teaspoon agave nectar

Classic Lemon Vinaigrette

ACTIVE TIME: 5 MINUTES • TOTAL TIME: 5 MINUTES • SERVING SIZE: ¾ CUP

Light, crisp, refreshing—this aromatic vinaigrette brings a citrus undertone to any bold flavors.

INGREDIENTS:

3 tablespoons lemon juice, freshly squeezed

Zest of ½ lemon

½ cup extra virgin olive oil

½ teaspoon sea salt

½ teaspoon black pepper, freshly ground

1 teaspoon honey

1 Zest the lemon before juicing.

2 Whisk all the ingredients in a small bowl or shake them in a jar and serve.

> IF YOU'RE LOOKING FOR SOMETHING LIGHTER AND LESS OVERPOWERING, SUBSTITUTE ACACIA HONEY FOR THE REGULAR STUFF.

No-Vinegar Vinaigrette

ACTIVE TIME: 5 MINUTES • TOTAL TIME: 5 MINUTES • SERVING SIZE: ½ CUP

This dressing is for when I do not want that sharp, acidic bite. It plays nicely with a big bowl of fresh cut vegetables, allowing the flavors of the veggies to shine through.

Whisk ingredients in a small bowl or shake them in a jar and serve.

INGREDIENTS:

½ cup extra virgin olive oil

1 teaspoon red chili flakes

1 teaspoon sea salt

1 teaspoon black pepper, freshly ground

Oregano Vinaigrette

ACTIVE TIME: 5 MINUTES • TOTAL TIME: 5 MINUTES • SERVING SIZE: ¾ CUP

Fresh or dried, oregano has a strong flavor perfect for Greek and Mediterranean salads. I love using this vinaigrette for a plate of fresh feta and olives. It boosts flavors and makes for a gorgeous presentation.

INGREDIENTS:

2 tablespoons red wine vinegar

1 tablespoon lemon juice, freshly squeezed

½ cup olive oil

1 teaspoon dry oregano, warmed in hands

½ shallot, minced

½ teaspoon sea salt

½ teaspoon black pepper, freshly ground

Whisk ingredients in a small bowl or shake them in a jar and serve.

Red Raspberry Vinaigrette

ACTIVE TIME: 5 MINUTES • TOTAL TIME: 5 MINUTES • SERVING SIZE: ¾ CUP

Crushed raspberries give this dressing a burst of color and sweetness, pairing nicely with the champagne vinegar to create a delicate and impressive topping.

Whisk ingredients in a small bowl or shake them in a jar and serve.

INGREDIENTS:

3 tablespoons champagne vinegar

½ cup extra virgin olive oil

½ cup fresh raspberries, mashed with fork

1 teaspoon sea salt

1 teaspoon black pepper, freshly ground

1 teaspoon honey

Strawberry Vinaigrette

ACTIVE TIME: 5 MINUTES • TOTAL TIME: 5 MINUTES • SERVING SIZE: ¾ CUP

This fruity delight makes the perfect accompaniment to any summer salad, but I won't tell anyone if you want to make it all year long. In fact, I encourage it!

INGREDIENTS:

3 tablespoons lemon juice, freshly squeezed

½ cup extra virgin olive oil

½ cup fresh strawberries, mashed with fork or pureed

1 teaspoon sea salt

1 teaspoon black pepper, freshly ground

1 teaspoon agave nectar

Whisk ingredients in a small bowl or shake them in a jar and serve.

Vinaigrettes

Lemon-Thyme Dressing

ACTIVE TIME: 5 MINUTES • TOTAL TIME: 5 MINUTES • SERVING SIZE: ¾ CUP

While this recipe calls for classic fresh thyme, I recently discovered a new strain of thyme called lemon thyme. Its mellow citrus flavor adds a new dimension to your salad—try it out for a fun variation!

Whisk ingredients in a small bowl or shake them in a jar and serve.

INGREDIENTS:

3 tablespoons lemon juice, freshly squeezed

½ cup extra virgin olive oil

2 tablespoons fresh thyme, finely chopped

1 teaspoon salt

1 teaspoon black pepper, freshly ground

1 teaspoon lemon zest

Lemon-Rosemary Dressing

While this goes well with any salad, it's perfect with some fresh bread and mozzarella. In fact, any Italian dish will agree with this classic flavor pairing.

INGREDIENTS:

3 tablespoons lemon juice, freshly squeezed

½ cup extra virgin olive oil

2 tablespoons fresh rosemary

½ clove garlic

1 teaspoon salt

1 teaspoon black pepper, freshly ground

1 Mince the garlic clove and then sprinkle the garlic pile with salt. Chop through one more time.

2 Using the back of your knife, squish the garlic into a paste. This ensures the garlic will mix evenly with the dressing, rather than show up randomly.

3 Whisk the ingredients in a small bowl or shake them in a jar and serve.

Parsley-Mint Vinaigrette

Mint and parsley aren't just for garnishing shrimp cocktail and desserts. Add these vibrant herbs to your dressing for a distinct flavor that will impress your taste buds—and your friends.

Whisk all ingredients in a small bowl until mixture has emulsified.

INGREDIENTS:

1 clove garlic, minced

1 cup flat-leaf parsley, finely chopped

¼ cup mint leaves, finely chopped

2 anchovies, minced

3 tablespoons lemon juice, freshly squeezed

½ cup extra virgin olive oil

1 teaspoon salt

1 teaspoon black pepper, freshly ground

Basil-Cilantro Vinaigrette

I love this vinaigrette for its zesty kick and fresh flavors. I fall into food ruts pretty often but this go-to dressing is always a great spark for my kitchen creativity.

INGREDIENTS:

½ cup cilantro, chopped

½ cup basil, chopped

2 tablespoons flat-leaf parsley, chopped

1 clove of garlic, minced

2 tablespoons jalapeño, finely chopped

2 tablespoons fresh lime or lemon juice

⅓ cup extra virgin olive oil

1 teaspoon black pepper, freshly ground

1 teaspoon salt

Whisk ingredients in a small bowl or shake them in a jar and serve.

Provençal Vinaigrette

ACTIVE TIME: 5 MINUTES • TOTAL TIME: 5 MINUTES • SERVING SIZE: ¾ CUP

While living in Provence for six months I finally discovered Herbs de Provence. Although the blend is not always the same, its most well known components are thyme, rosemary, savory, oregano, marjoram and lavender; together, they blend to create an entirely new spice. When tossed on your favorite Provençal-style salad or drizzled over any cut of meat, this dressing takes you right to the hillsides of Southern France.

Whisk the ingredients in a small bowl or shake them in a jar and serve.

INGREDIENTS:

1 teaspoon dried herbs de Provence, warmed in hands

4 tablespoons white wine vinegar

½ cup olive oil

½ small clove garlic, crushed and finely chopped

¼ teaspoon black pepper, freshly ground

¼ teaspoon salt

Citrus Vinaigrette

This Florida-inspired dressing is as visually pleasing as it is flavorful!

INGREDIENTS:

1 tablespoon lemon juice, freshly squeezed

1 tablespoon lime juice, freshly squeezed

1 tablespoon orange juice, freshly squeezed

½ cup olive oil

1 teaspoon salt

½ teaspoon black pepper, freshly ground

½ teaspoon of lemon, lime and orange zest

Whisk ingredients in a small bowl or shake them in a jar and serve.

Garlic-Lemon-Oregano Vinaigrette

ACTIVE TIME: 5 MINUTES • TOTAL TIME: 5 MINUTES • SERVING SIZE: ¾ CUP

Garlic, lemon and oregano go so well together that a little bit of this combination will have even the biggest salad-haters reaching for the tongs.

1 Add the garlic, anchovies and red pepper flakes to a food processor. Pulse 2 or 3 times.

2 Add the oregano and chopped lemon and pulse. Stream in olive oil until pureed.

3 Add salt, black pepper and lemon juice, to taste.

INGREDIENTS:

2 cloves garlic, chopped

2 anchovy fillets, packed in oil and drained

¾ teaspoon red pepper flakes, crushed

2 tablespoons lemon juice, freshly squeezed

½ lemon, finely chopped

¼ cup fresh oregano leaves, loosely packed

¼ cup extra virgin olive oil

Pinch of salt, if necessary

Creamy Dijon Vinaigrette

If you want to get kooky, try this as a marinade next time you grill salmon and thank me later.

INGREDIENTS:

3 tablespoons white wine vinegar

1 tablespoon Dijon mustard

½ teaspoon granulated sugar

½ teaspoon salt

½ teaspoon black pepper, freshly ground

½ clove garlic

½ cup extra virgin olive oil

Blend all ingredients until they are creamy and emulsified.

REPLACE THE DIJON WITH GRAINY MUSTARD FOR ADDED TEXTURE AND A SHARPER FLAVOR!

Bacon Vinaigrette

ACTIVE TIME: 10 MINUTES • TOTAL TIME: 10 MINUTES • SERVING SIZE: ¾ CUP

Savory, salty, smoky—in a dressing, a little bacon goes a long way. And no matter your cooking experience, you don't need me to tell you that bacon makes any dish an indulgent treat.

INGREDIENTS:

2 tablespoons bacon drippings

¼ cup extra virgin olive oil

3 tablespoons apple cider vinegar

1 tablespoon Dijon mustard

2 teaspoons light brown sugar

1 teaspoon black pepper, freshly ground

Salt, to taste

1 For the bacon drippings: Cook 5 pieces of thick-cut bacon in frying pan until crispy. Remove bacon from pan and add 2 tablespoons of slightly cooled drippings to a bowl.

2 Whisk ingredients in a small bowl or shake them in a jar and serve.

> TIP: TO REALLY INDULGE, COOK SOME HOMEMADE SOURDOUGH CROUTONS IN THE LEFTOVER BACON DRIPPINGS AND USE THE BACON FOR YOUR SALAD!

Chipotle and Adobo Vinaigrette

ACTIVE TIME: 5 MINUTES • TOTAL TIME: 5 MINUTES • SERVING SIZE: ¾ CUP

These rich and smoky peppers are perfect for any southwestern-inspired dish.

Whisk ingredients in a small bowl or shake them in a jar and serve.

INGREDIENTS:

½ cup vegetable oil

2 tablespoons white wine vinegar

2 chipotles in adobo

1 teaspoon of adobo sauce

½ teaspoon salt

½ teaspoon black pepper, freshly ground

1 teaspoon honey,

1 teaspoon Dijon mustard

1 tablespoon freshly squeezed lime juice

Honey–Black Pepper Vinaigrette

Sweet and spicy perfection for the pepper-lovers of the world!

INGREDIENTS:

¼ cup sherry vinegar

2 tablespoons honey, warmed for easy mixing

1 tablespoon black pepper, freshly ground

1 teaspoon salt

1 shallot, minced

1 clove garlic, minced

1 cup of olive oil

¼ cup fresh mint leaves, torn

Combine everything in a jar. Tightly seal the lid and shake until the mixture is creamy.

Pear-Balsamic Vinaigrette

ACTIVE TIME: 5 MINUTES • **TOTAL TIME: 5 MINUTES** • **SERVING SIZE: ¾ CUP**

Elegant and easy, these two distinct flavors combine to make an autumnal delight.

Whisk ingredients in a small bowl or shake them in a jar and serve.

IF YOU CAN'T FIND ANY GORGONZOLA, ANOTHER BLUE CHEESE WILL DO. JUST MAKE SURE IT'S THE CRUMBLY STUFF!

INGREDIENTS:

⅓ cup extra virgin olive oil

3 tablespoons pear nectar

2 tablespoons white balsamic vinegar

½ tablespoon lemon juice

¼ teaspoon Dijon mustard

¼ teaspoon kosher salt

¼ teaspoon black pepper, freshly ground

½ cup crumbled Gorgonzola

Anchovy-Date Dressing

This intriguing combination is sure to surprise even the most jaded salad-eaters. (In a good way, of course.)

INGREDIENTS:

4 large dates, pitted and finely chopped

8 anchovy fillets, finely chopped

1 orange, zested and juiced

1 clove of garlic, minced

⅓ cup olive oil

2 tablespoons sherry vinegar

1 teaspoon black pepper, freshly ground

1 With a fork, mash the dates, anchovies, garlic and orange zest in the bowl.

2 Mix in oil, orange juice and vinegar and whisk until blended evenly. Be sure to add the oil slowly!

Red Onion Vinaigrette

ACTIVE TIME: 10 MINUTES • TOTAL TIME: 10 MINUTES • SERVING SIZE: ¾ CUP

This classic vinaigrette makes a lovely accompaniment to a weekend brunch salad.

1 Soak red onion in water for 5–7 minutes to diminish its sharp bite.

2 Once your onion is chopped, combine ingredients in a jar and shake until blended evenly.

INGREDIENTS:

2 teaspoons olive oil

1 medium red onion, thinly sliced

1 clove garlic, minced

½ teaspoon fresh thyme leaves

½ cup extra virgin olive oil

¼ cup cider vinegar

2 tablespoons white balsamic vinegar

4 teaspoons honey

1 teaspoon salt

1 teaspoon black pepper, freshly ground

Tarragon Vinaigrette

Tarragon—the most elegant herb, for my money—carries just hint of anise flavor and can elevate any dish. I like using this vinaigrette on weeknight chicken to spice things up.

INGREDIENTS:

2 cloves garlic, minced

1 teaspoon Dijon mustard

3 tablespoons red wine vinegar

1 tablespoon lemon juice, freshly squeezed

2 tablespoons flat-leaf parsley, chopped

2 tablespoons fresh tarragon, minced

1 teaspoon sea salt

1 teaspoon black pepper, freshly ground

½ cup extra virgin olive oil

Whisk ingredients in a small bowl or shake them in a jar and serve.

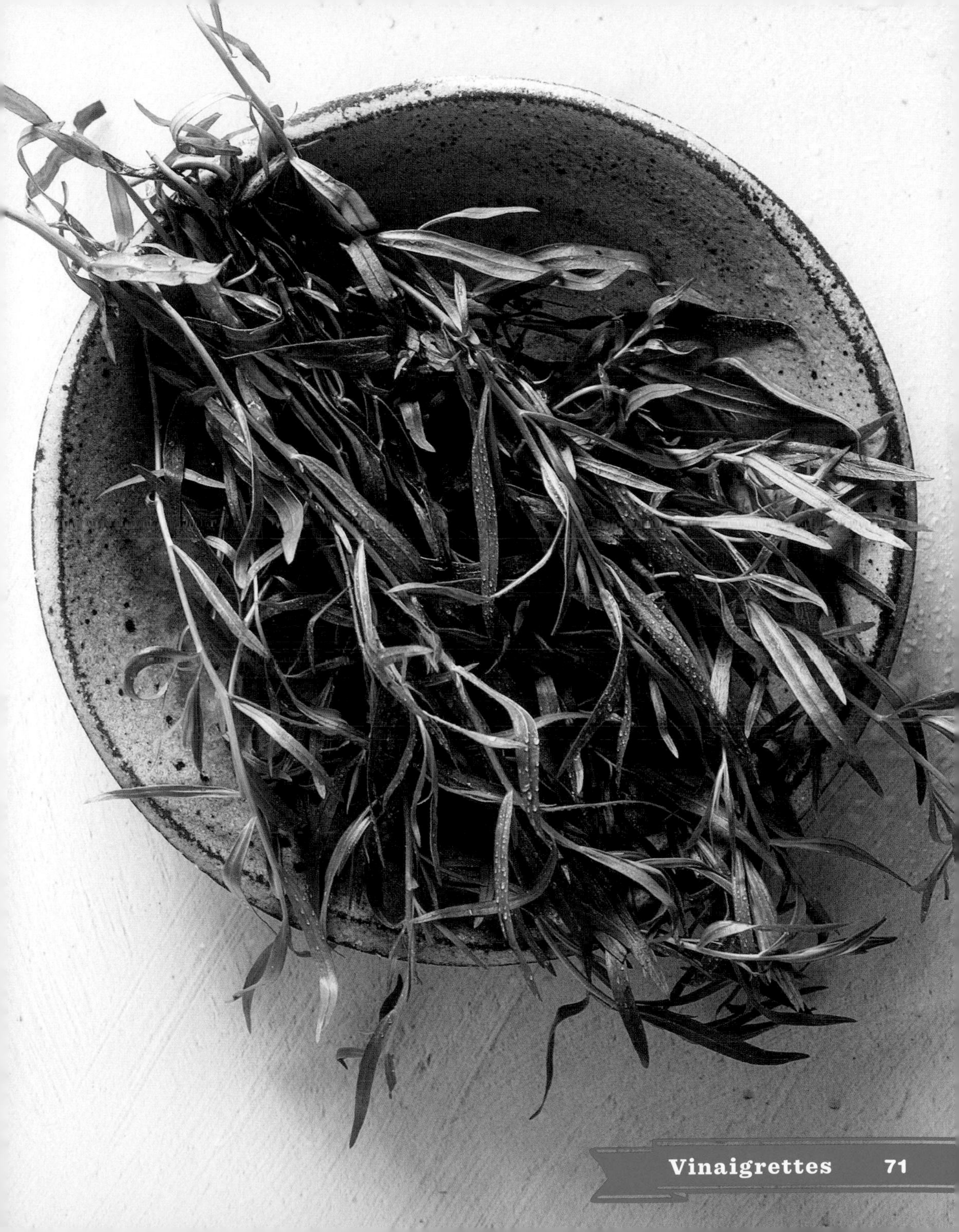

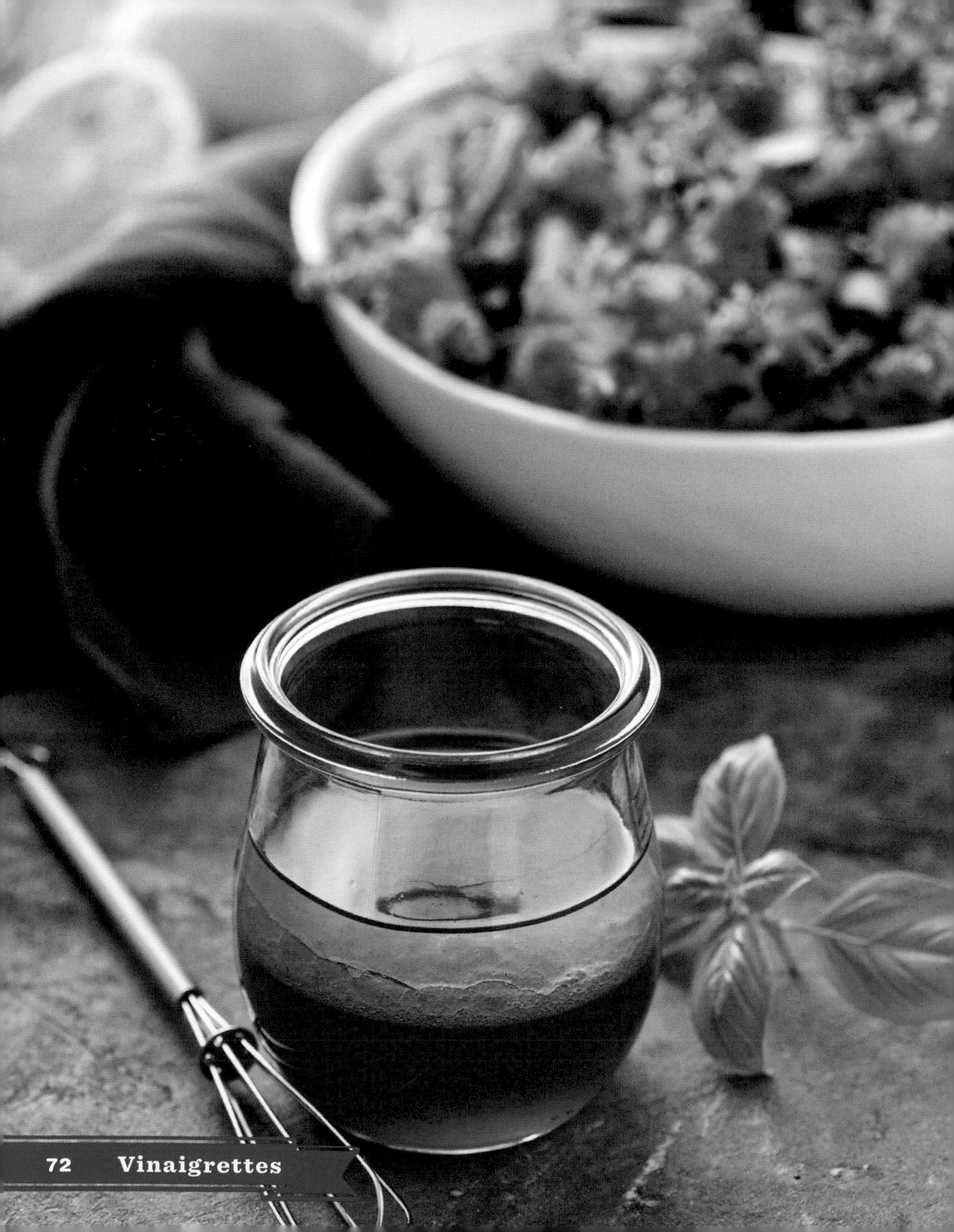

Pomegranate Vinaigrette

Invest in a bottle of this trendy ingredient and enjoy its tasty benefits for as long as you can make it last—beginning with this exotic spin on a classic recipe.

Whisk ingredients in a small bowl or shake them in a jar and serve.

INGREDIENTS:

¼ cup pomegranate molasses

2 tablespoons red wine vinegar

1 tablespoon Dijon mustard

1 tablespoon honey

1 teaspoon salt

1 teaspoon black pepper, freshly ground

¾ cup extra virgin olive oil

Sweet and Sour Dressing

ACTIVE TIME: 5 MINUTES • TOTAL TIME: 5 MINUTES • SERVING SIZE: ¾ CUP

This dressing is so versatile—it can be used as a marinade, dressing or dipping sauce for any of your favorite Asian-inspired dishes.

INGREDIENTS:

1 clove garlic, minced

¼ cup lime juice

2 tablespoons orange juice

2 tablespoons fish sauce

2 teaspoons rice wine vinegar

2 tablespoons honey

½ teaspoon Sriracha, adjusting to taste

Shake the ingredients in a jar until they've mixed evenly.

Crème Fraiche Vinaigrette

Toss this creamy and decadent vinaigrette over cooked potatoes, steamed vegetables or roasted beets. Perfection.

Whisk ingredients in a small bowl or shake them in a jar and serve.

INGREDIENTS:

½ cup crème fraiche

¼ cup extra virgin olive oil

2 tablespoons champagne vinegar

1 tablespoons honey

½ teaspoon salt

¼ teaspoon black pepper, freshly ground

Lemon-Dill Vinaigrette

A light topping for springtime vegetables like asparagus, peas and mushrooms. Or toss with potatoes for a lighter take on potato salad.

INGREDIENTS:

3 tablespoons lemon juice, freshly squeezed

Zest of ½ lemon

½ cup extra virgin olive oil

½ teaspoon sea salt

½ teaspoon black pepper, freshly ground

1 teaspoon honey

2 tablespoons fresh dill

Whisk ingredients in a small bowl or shake them in a jar and serve.

Fennel–Blood Orange Vinaigrette

ACTIVE TIME: 5 MINUTES • TOTAL TIME: 5 MINUTES • SERVING SIZE: ¾ CUP

The perfect dressing to help you transition from summer to fall. Try this flavorful vinaigrette over hardy greens, poultry or pork.

Whisk ingredients in a small bowl or shake them in a jar and serve.

INGREDIENTS:

3 tablespoons blood orange juice, freshly squeezed

2 teaspoons white wine vinegar

1 teaspoon roasted fennel seeds, crushed

¼ teaspoon blood orange zest

¼ teaspoon black pepper, freshly ground

2 tablespoons olive oil

1 teaspoon salt

Roasted Red Pepper Vinaigrette

ACTIVE TIME: 5 MINUTES • TOTAL TIME: 5 MINUTES • SERVING SIZE: ¾ CUP

This is a favorite of mine, especially when accompanying a toasted baguette with fresh goat cheese.

INGREDIENTS:

3 tablespoons lemon juice, freshly squeezed

Zest of ½ lemon

½ cup extra virgin olive oil

½ teaspoon sea salt

½ teaspoon black pepper, freshly ground

1 teaspoon honey

1 cup roasted red pepper, cut into strips

1 teaspoon fresh rosemary

Combine all ingredients in a blender and blend until smooth. If the mixture is looking a bit thick, add water to attain proper consistency.

Sally's Roasted Tomato Dressing

ACTIVE TIME: 20 MINUTES • TOTAL TIME: 30 MINUTES • SERVING SIZE: 1 CUP

I love to toss this tasty dressing with pasta or a romaine-based salad, sprinkle with Parmesan and serve.

1 Preheat your oven to 425 degrees Fahrenheit. In an ovenproof baking dish, toss the cherry tomatoes and shallots in 2 tablespoons of olive oil, salt and pepper. Pour in ¼ cup balsamic vinegar.

2 Bake for 20–25 minutes or until slightly charred and wilted, stirring once halfway through.

3 After you've removed the dish, toss the mixture in the remaining 2 tablespoons of extra virgin olive oil, 1 tablespoon of balsamic vinegar and the rest of the pepper. Optional: garnish with rosemary.

INGREDIENTS:

1 pint of cherry tomatoes

4 tablespoons extra virgin olive oil

¼ cup and 1 tablespoon balsamic vinegar, separated

2 shallots minced

1 teaspoon sea salt

2 teaspoons black pepper, freshly ground

1 sprig rosemary (optional)

Pecorino Romano and Black Pepper Vinaigrette

ACTIVE TIME: 5 MINUTES • TOTAL TIME: 5 MINUTES • SERVING SIZE: ¾ CUP

This is my take on the classic cacio e pepe pasta dish. Toss it over fresh greens or any cooked vegetable for a cheesy delight.

INGREDIENTS:

¼ cup fresh lemon juice

⅓ cup olive oil

½ cup Pecorino Romano, freshly grated

1 clove garlic, smashed for added flavor

2 teaspoons black pepper, freshly ground

½ teaspoon salt

Whisk all ingredients in a small bowl until mixture has emulsified, making sure to pour the oil slowly.

Chimichurri Vinaigrette

ACTIVE TIME: 5 MINUTES • TOTAL TIME: 5 MINUTES • SERVING SIZE: 1 CUP

Inspired by the South American sauce, this vinaigrette is made for sliced steak over a bed of spring greens.

Whisk ingredients in a small bowl or shake them in a jar and serve.

INGREDIENTS:

½ cup red wine vinegar

2 cloves garlic, minced

1 small shallot, minced

1 scallion, minced

1 serrano chile, minced (red for added color)

1 tablespoon lime juice, freshly squeezed

1 teaspoon salt

½ cup flat-leaf parsley, minced

½ cup cilantro, minced

¾ cup extra virgin olive oil

Herbaceous Vinaigrette

ACTIVE TIME: 5 MINUTES • TOTAL TIME: 5 MINUTES • SERVING SIZE: ¾ CUP

When your window garden is at its peak, harvest your tiny bounty for this fragrant treat.

INGREDIENTS:

¼ cup red wine vinegar

½ clove garlic, minced

1 teaspoon fresh oregano leaves, chopped

1 teaspoon fresh thyme leaves, chopped

1 teaspoon fresh parsley leaves, chopped

1 teaspoon salt

½ teaspoon black pepper, freshly ground

¾ cup extra virgin olive oil

Whisk ingredients in a small bowl or shake them in a jar and serve.

Kalamata Olive Vinaigrette

ACTIVE TIME: 5 MINUTES • TOTAL TIME: 5 MINUTES • SERVING SIZE: ¾ CUP

If you love tapenade like I do, make this salty dressing to drizzle over crostini with ricotta cheese or a Greek-style pasta salad.

Combine all ingredients in blender and blend until smooth.

IF YOU WANT TO MAKE YOUR DRESSING MORE COLORFUL WITHOUT SIGNIFICANTLY DISTURBING ITS FLAVOR, USE GREEN MANZANILLA OLIVES.

INGREDIENTS:

3 tablespoons lemon juice, freshly squeezed

½ cup extra virgin olive oil

2 tablespoons fresh thyme, finely chopped

1 teaspoon salt

1 teaspoon black pepper, freshly ground

1 teaspoon lemon zest

½ cup pitted Kalamata olives

Garlic Confit Vinaigrette

ACTIVE TIME: 20 MINUTES • TOTAL TIME: 40 MINUTES • SERVING SIZE: 1½ CUPS

Perfect for garlic lovers to use on winter salads or a well-grilled steak.

INGREDIENTS:

For garlic confit:

8 cloves garlic, peeled and de-stemmed (if necessary)

3 sprigs fresh thyme and rosemary

1½ cups olive oil

For the vinaigrette:

8 cloves garlic confit (see above)

¼ cup white wine vinegar

1 tablespoon lemon juice, freshly squeezed

½ cup garlic-infused olive oil

½ teaspoon salt

1 teaspoon black pepper, freshly ground

1 To make your garlic confit, add the designated ingredients in a pan and cook over very low heat for 30 minutes so as not to burn the garlic and herbs. Stir occasionally. Everything should be golden brown and tender when finished.

2 Once your confit is finished, turn the heat off and mash the garlic in the pan. Add salt when your mixture is sufficiently smooth.

3 Whisk in oil, lemon juice and vinegar until blended evenly, making sure to add them slowly. When the mixture has emulsified, add black pepper to taste.

Black Truffle Vinaigrette

ACTIVE TIME: 5 MINUTES • TOTAL TIME: 5 MINUTES • SERVING SIZE: ¾ CUP

Trendy and impressive, truffles are great if you want give company a pleasant surprise. Just be careful when using the truffle oil, as it tends to be a very overpowering flavor—use it sparingly until you've tasted the vinaigrette.

Whisk ingredients in a small bowl or shake them in a jar and serve.

INGREDIENTS:

1 tablespoon Dijon mustard

1 tablespoon champagne vinegar

1 shallot, minced

½ teaspoon salt

1 teaspoon pepper

¼ cup black truffle oil

⅓ cup olive oil

Melon-Mint Vinaigrette

For a burst of color and flavor, pour this dressing over your delicate summer greens as a refreshing snack or side. This even works drizzled over burrata or fresh mozzarella.

INGREDIENTS:

½ cantaloupe, grated and drained of excess water

¼ cup extra virgin olive oil

2 tablespoons white wine vinegar

1 teaspoon black pepper, freshly ground

2 tablespoons fresh mint leaves, chopped

Whisk ingredients in a small bowl or shake them in a jar and serve.

Spiced Chutney Vinaigrette

ACTIVE TIME: 5 MINUTES • TOTAL TIME: 5 MINUTES • SERVING SIZE: ¾ CUP

This dressing adds warmth to any fall-inspired salad. Use hardy leaves like kale or mustard greens to stand up to this big dressing.

Whisk ingredients in a small bowl or shake them in a jar and serve.

INGREDIENTS:

2 tablespoons mango chutney

2 tablespoons lime juice, freshly squeezed

½ teaspoon cumin

1 teaspoon salt

¼ cup vegetable oil

Orange-Walnut Vinaigrette

ACTIVE TIME: 5 MINUTES • TOTAL TIME: 5 MINUTES • SERVING SIZE: ¾ CUP

For extra crunch in this nutty topping, add chopped unsalted walnuts. You can lightly toast them in a dry skillet to bring out their flavor.

INGREDIENTS:

2 tablespoons orange juice

1 tablespoon sherry vinegar

½ teaspoon salt

½ teaspoon black pepper, freshly ground

⅓ cup walnut oil

⅓ cup olive oil

Whisk ingredients in a small bowl or shake them in a jar and serve.

Apple Dressing

This dressing is perfect for a light coleslaw, but I suspect even the slaw-averse will find use for it at their next barbecue.

Whisk ingredients in a small bowl or shake them in a jar and serve.

INGREDIENTS:

½ cup apple juice

¼ cup apple cider vinegar

1 clove garlic, minced

1 tablespoon soy sauce

1 teaspoon Worcestershire sauce

2 teaspoons olive oil

1 teaspoon black pepper, freshly ground

Piquillo Pepper Vinaigrette

A Spanish chili pepper that possesses little to no spiciness, piquillos carry a sweet flavor closest to that of a bell pepper.

INGREDIENTS:

5 piquillo peppers, chopped

½ small red onion, coarsely chopped

8 cloves roasted garlic, peeled

¼ cup sherry vinegar

1 tablespoon honey

1 tablespoon Dijon mustard

1 teaspoon salt

1 teaspoon black pepper, freshly ground

½ cup canola oil

Whisk ingredients in a small bowl or shake them in a jar and serve.

Poppy Seed Vinaigrette

Poppy seeds aren't just for bagels, you know. Use them in this fun dressing to make a more whimsical salad. I enjoy this one over butter lettuce, strawberries and goat cheese.

1 Toast the poppy seeds in dry skillet over medium heat for 1 minute.

2 Whisk ingredients in a small bowl or shake them in a jar and serve.

INGREDIENTS:

½ tablespoon poppy seeds

3 tablespoons apple cider vinegar

1 tablespoon honey

1 teaspoon Dijon mustard

½ teaspoon salt

⅓ cup olive oil

Creamy Dressings

If you're a fan of Caesar, ranch, blue cheese—really, any kind of cheese—then this is the section for you. Here you will discover lush, creamy dressings that are sure to satisfy your craving. In fact, homemade Caesar dressing is one of the recipes that inspired this book. The first Caesar I ever had was my mom's; I had no idea she made her own until I tasted the store-bought version and realized how much I preferred the stuff she'd be serving for years. The nuanced combination of anchovies, garlic and fresh Parmesan just wasn't the same.

Very similar concepts apply to the other creamy recipes found in this chapter. You really cannot beat fresh ranch dressing or the flavor of real blue cheese. And for so many salad-eaters, a flavorful creamy dressing can make all the difference between getting your nutrients and just pushing food around until the main course shows up. Whether you're using them as dressings or dipping sauces, these recipes are certain to please the masses.

Classic Caesar Dressing

ACTIVE TIME: 10 MINUTES • TOTAL TIME: 10 MINUTES • SERVING SIZE: ¾ CUP

You know the drill: Drizzle over romaine lettuce and fresh croutons. Top with fresh shavings of Parmesan cheese and enjoy!

Combine all the ingredients in a blender and puree until emulsified.

INGREDIENTS:

2 egg yolks

5 anchovy filets

3 cloves garlic, chopped

1½ teaspoons black pepper, freshly ground

¼ cup lemon juice

2–3 dashes of Worcestershire sauce

2 tablespoons sherry or red wine vinegar

1 tablespoon Dijon mustard

½ cup extra virgin olive oil

½ cup grated Parmesan cheese

1 teaspoon black pepper, freshly ground

FOR A SMOKY VARIATION OF THIS CLASSIC, JUST SUBSTITUTE ROASTED GARLIC FOR THE FRESH GARLIC. JUST LIKE THAT, YOU HAVE A ROASTED GARLIC CAESAR!

Eggless Caesar Dressing

ACTIVE TIME: 5 MINUTES • TOTAL TIME: 5 MINUTES • SERVING SIZE: ¾ CUP

For the many among us with egg allergies—and those who just hate eggs—here's an easy alternative that'll allow you to enjoy your Caesar salad in peace.

INGREDIENTS:

5 anchovy filets

3 cloves garlic, chopped

1½ teaspoons black pepper, freshly ground

¼ cup lemon juice

2 tablespoons sherry or red wine vinegar

1 tablespoon Dijon mustard

½ cup extra virgin olive oil

½ cup grated Parmesan cheese

Combine all ingredients in a blender and blend until emulsified.

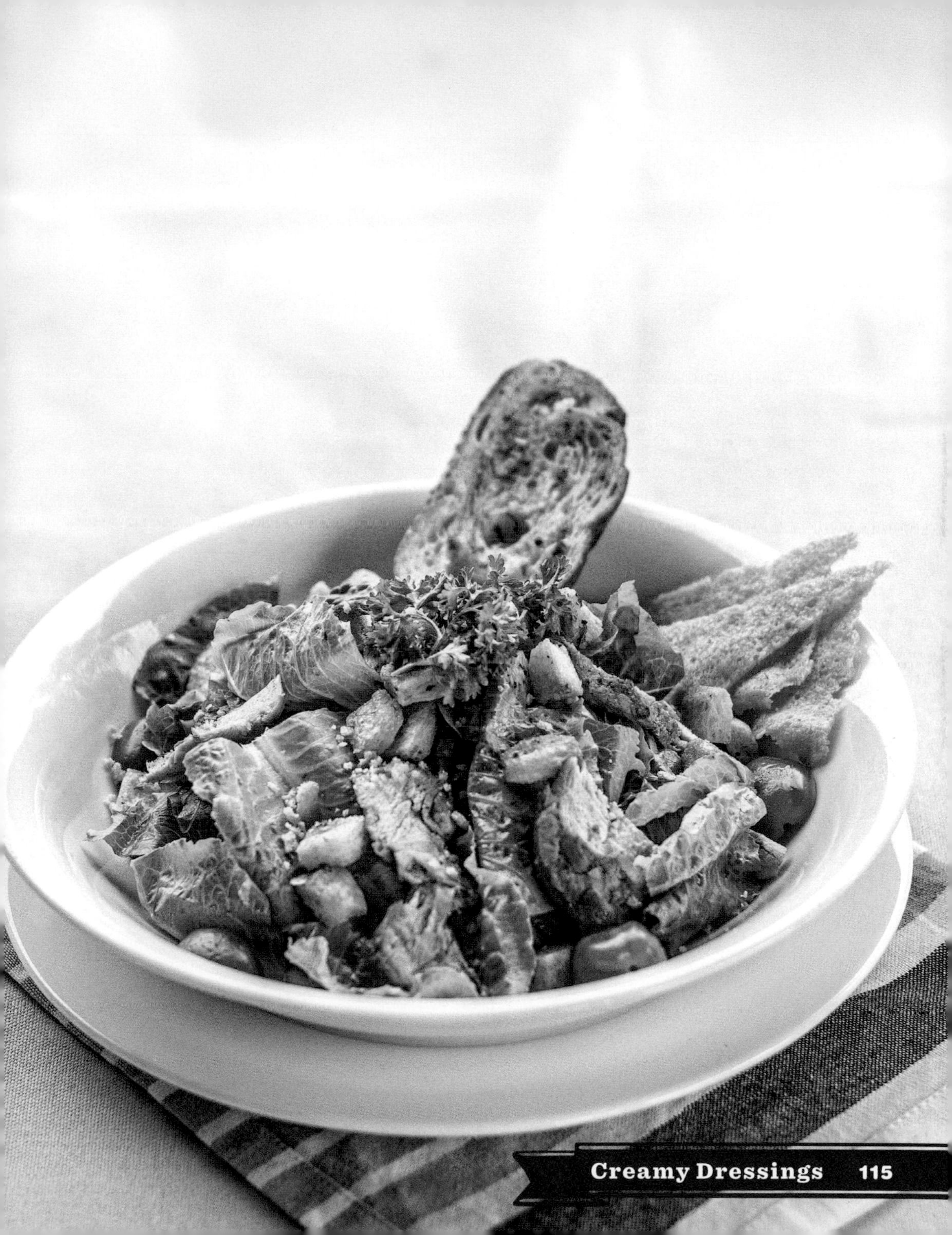

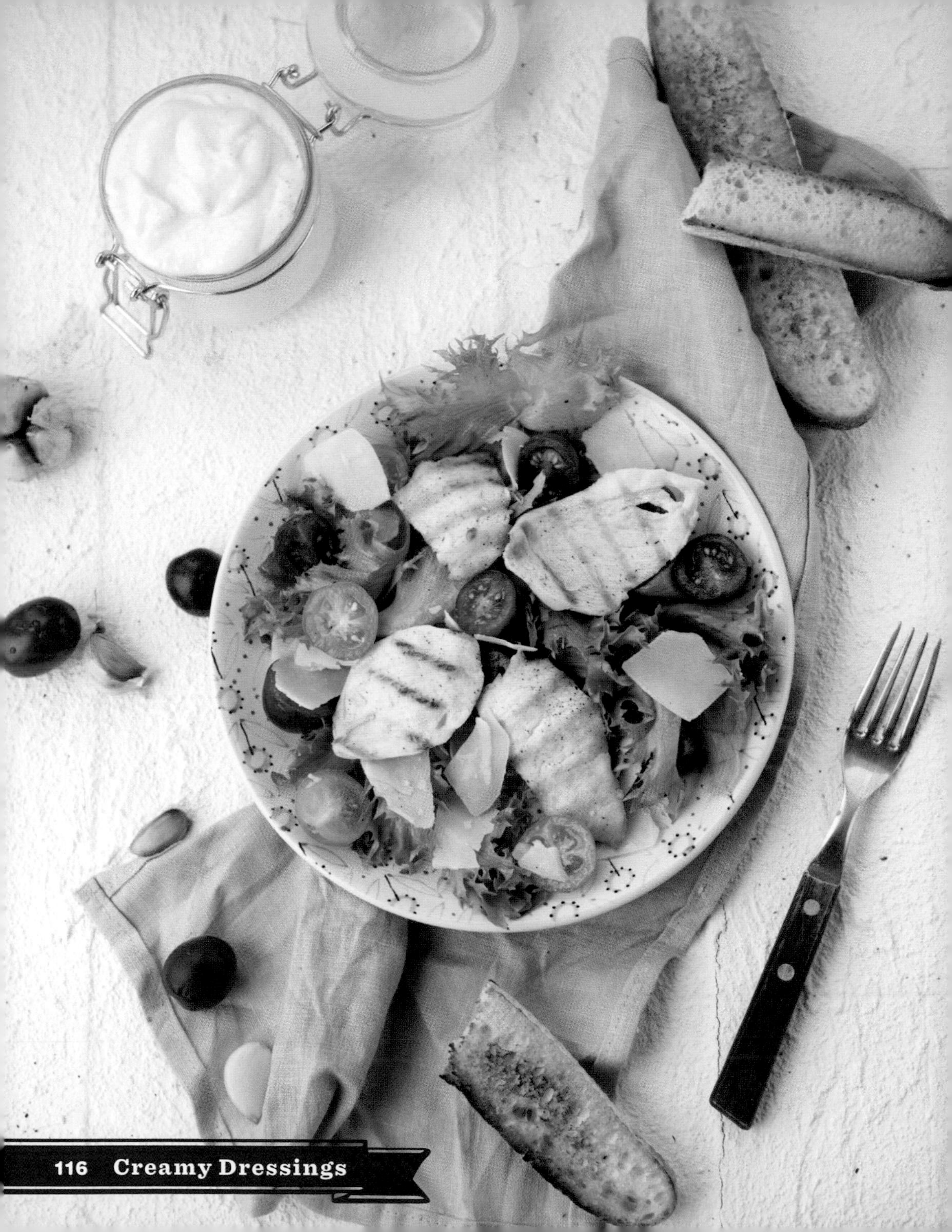

Light Caesar Dressing

½ cup nonfat Greek yogurt

2 tablespoons Parmesan, freshly grated

1 tablespoon olive oil

1 tablespoon water

1 clove garlic

2–3 dashes of Worcestershire

4 anchovies

2 tablespoons lemon juice, freshly squeezed

Cashew Caesar

I was surprised to learn that not many people have experienced a proper cashew-Caesar dressing, which is a shame because these flavors complement one another beautifully. Try this out and see if you prefer it to the old standby!

INGREDIENTS:

4 anchovies

¼ cup raw cashews

3 tablespoons fresh lemon juice

1 tablespoon Dijon mustard

2 teaspoons Worcestershire

½ cup olive oil

1 teaspoon salt

1 teaspoon black pepper, freshly ground

Combine all ingredients in a blender and blend until emulsified.

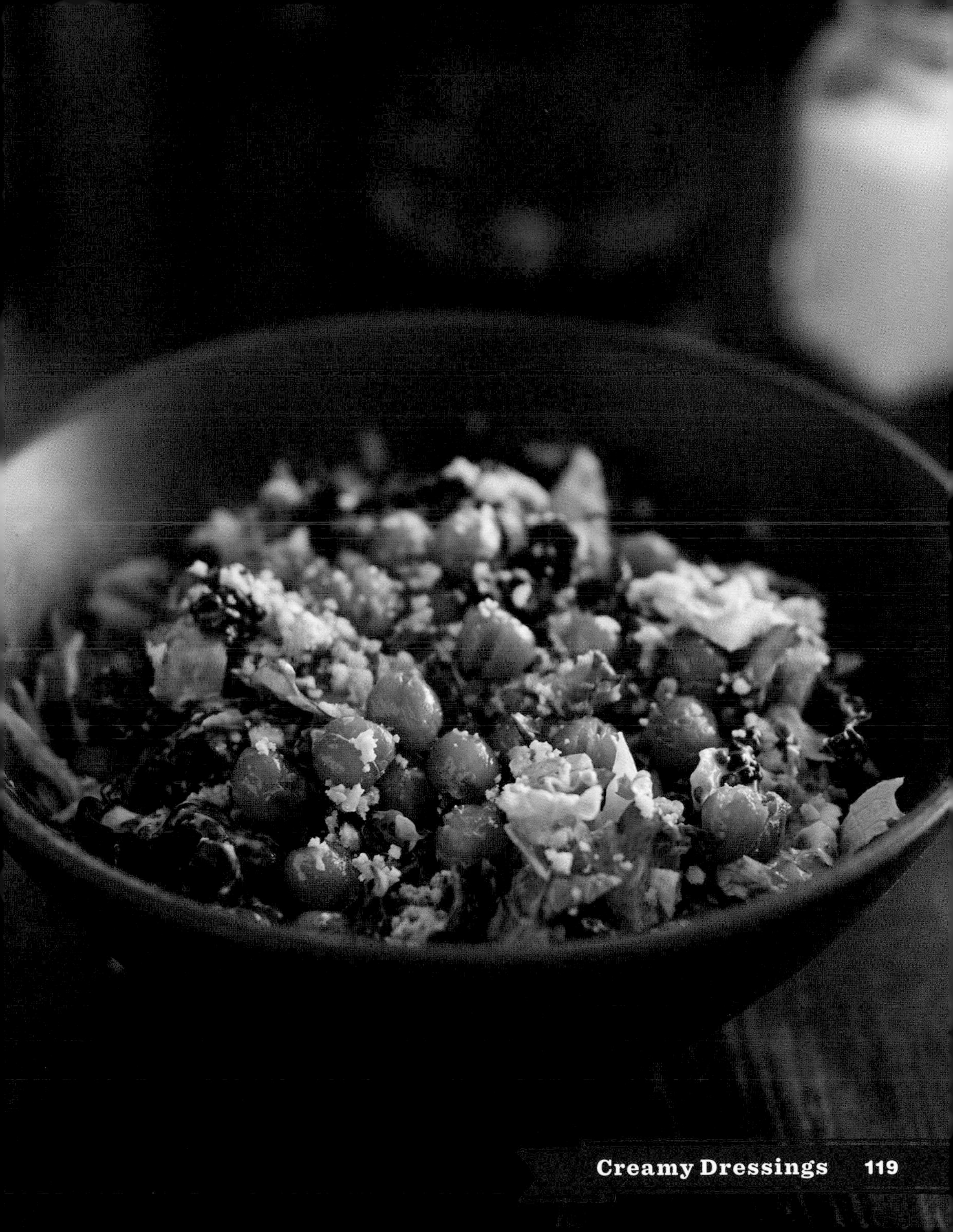

If you're reading a dressings book, chances are you've experienced the joy of ranch dressing before. Let me tell you: It's even better homemade. Enjoy this recipe with everything from baby carrots and snap peas to a chicken cutlet sandwich!

Whisk all the ingredients in bowl until they've emulsified.

INGREDIENTS:

- ½ cup buttermilk
- ½ cup mayonnaise
- ½ cup sour cream
- 2 tablespoons parsley, chopped
- 2 tablespoons chives, chopped
- 1 teaspoon apple-cider vinegar
- ½ teaspoon salt
- ½ teaspoon garlic powder
- ¼ teaspoon black pepper, freshly ground
- a dash of hot sauce

THIS RECIPE SERVES AS AN EASY BASE FOR TONS OF FUN VARIATIONS. A FEW OF MY FAVORITES:

- **LIGHT RANCH:** Replace the mayonnaise and sour cream with ½ cup of nonfat Greek yogurt and add ¼ teaspoon of sugar.

- **BACON RANCH:** Add 4 slices crispy bacon, crumbled.

- **EXTRA HERBY RANCH:** Add thyme, basil, oregano, chervil, to taste.

- **ROASTED GARLIC RANCH:** Add two cloves of roasted garlic.

Smoky Ranch

Add chipotle in adobo for this smoky Southwestern take on classic ranch.

INGREDIENTS

½ cup buttermilk

¼ cup mayonnaise

¼ cup sour cream

2 tablespoons lime juice, freshly squeezed

2 tablespoons chipotles in adobo sauce, chopped

2 tablespoons cilantro, chopped

½ teaspoon honey

½ teaspoon salt

⅛ teaspoon garlic powder

Whisk all ingredients together until mixed.

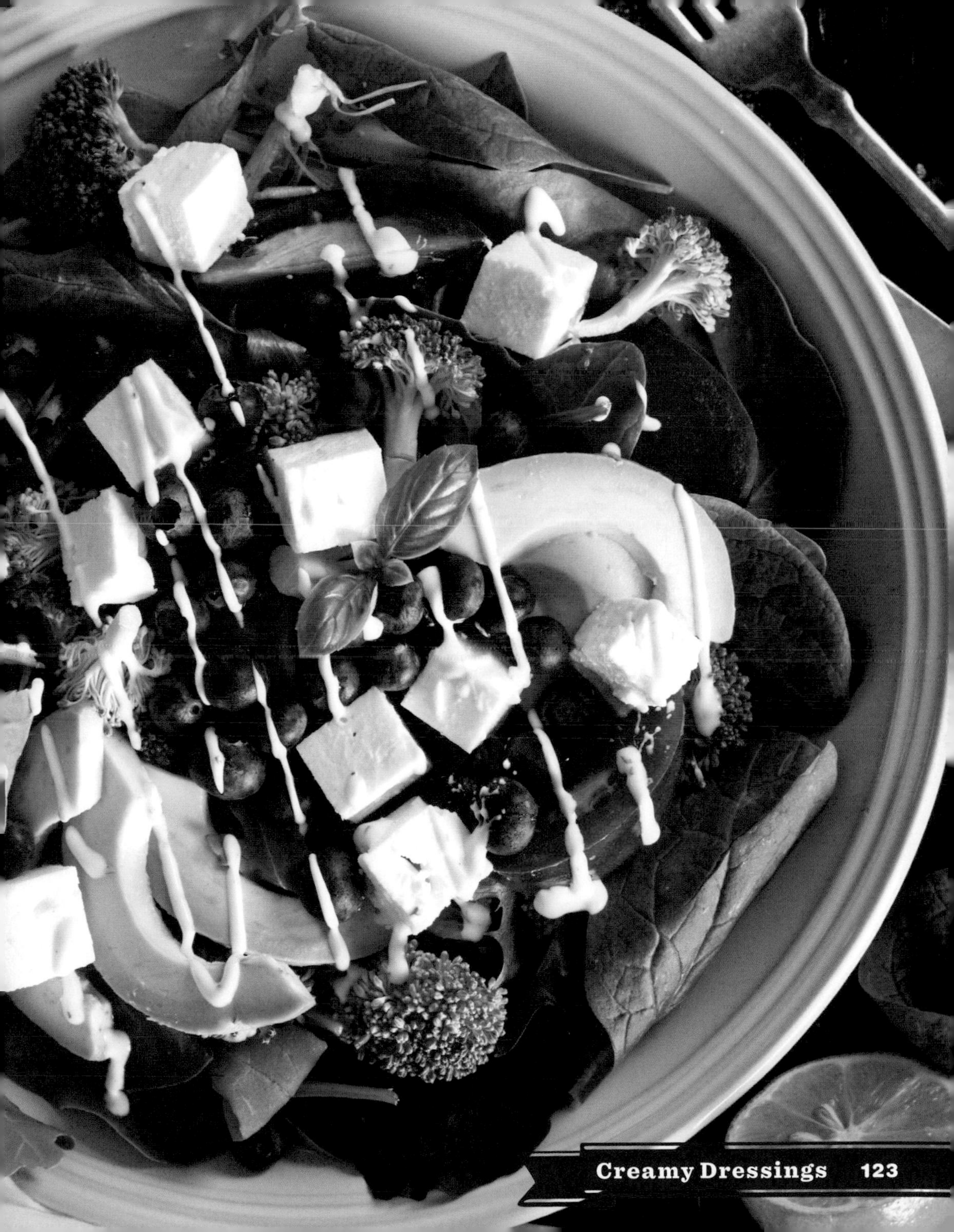

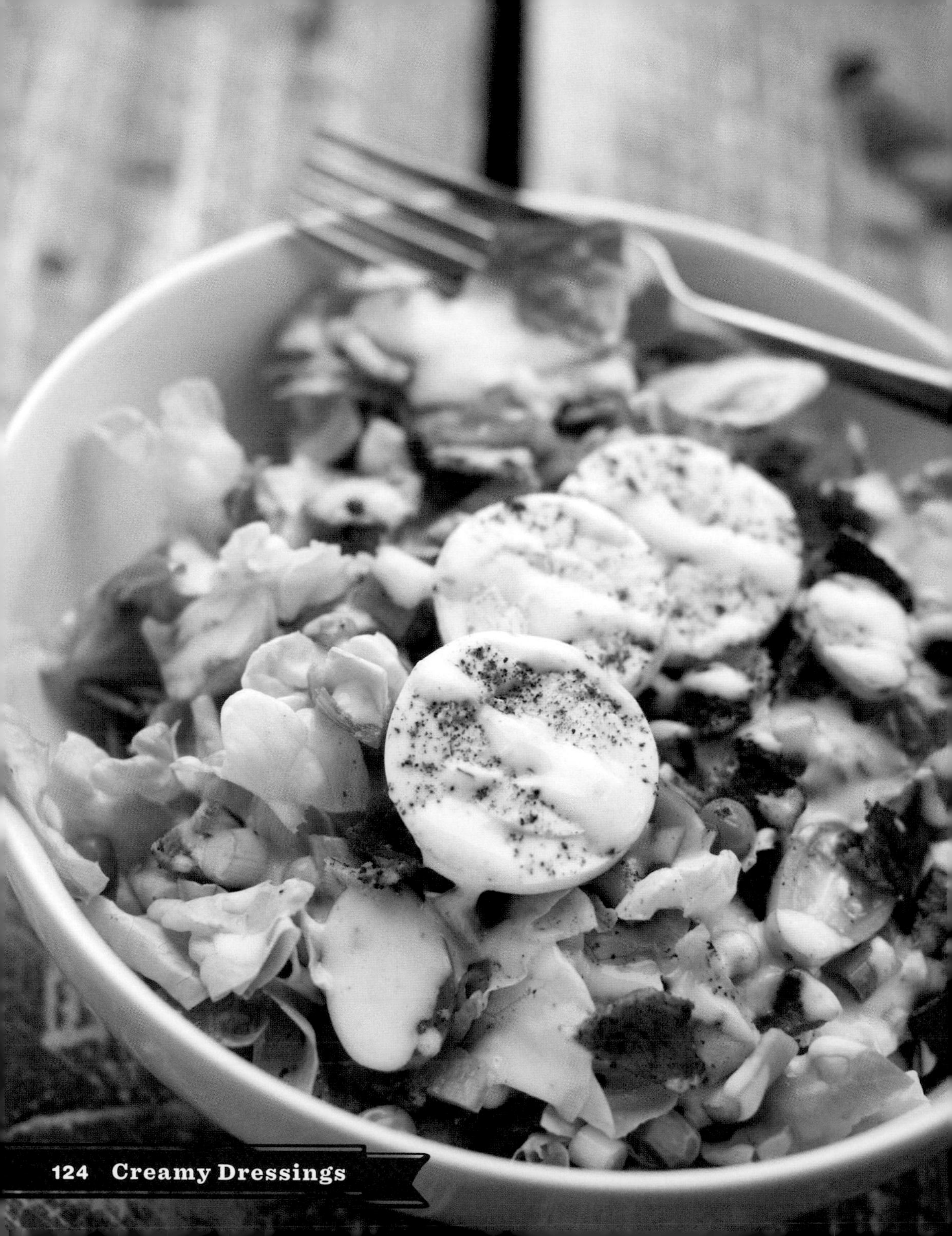

Tofu-Peppercorn Ranch

ACTIVE TIME: 10 MINUTES • **TOTAL TIME:** 10 MINUTES • **SERVING SIZE:** 1½ CUPS

A fresh way to use extra tofu, this recipe is perfect for vegetarians and tofu-lovers. This vegan ranch will have even the biggest dairy-lovers licking their chops.

Purée all the ingredients in a blender until smooth.

INGREDIENTS:

¾ cup vegan mayonnaise

½ cup plain soy yogurt

½ cup soft (silken) tofu

¼ cup unsweetened rice milk

3 tablespoons fresh lemon juice

1 tablespoon apple cider vinegar

1½ teaspoons white miso

¾ teaspoon black pepper, freshly ground

¾ teaspoon plum vinegar (optional)

½ teaspoon fresh tarragon

½ teaspoon garlic, minced

⅛ teaspoon mustard powder

1 teaspoon salt

Buttermilk Dressing

ACTIVE TIME: 5 MINUTES • TOTAL TIME: 5 MINUTES • SERVING SIZE: 1½ CUPS

Ah, buttermilk: the secret to baked goods, pancakes . . .and creamy dressing! This makes a tangy and refreshing topping for a bowl of Boston lettuce and fresh tomatoes.

INGREDIENTS:

½ cup buttermilk

½ cup mayonnaise

¼ cup sour cream

1 teaspoon white vinegar

1–2 dashes of hot sauce

1 clove garlic, pressed

1 teaspoon salt

1 teaspoon black pepper, freshly ground

Whisk all the ingredients in bowl until they've emulsified.

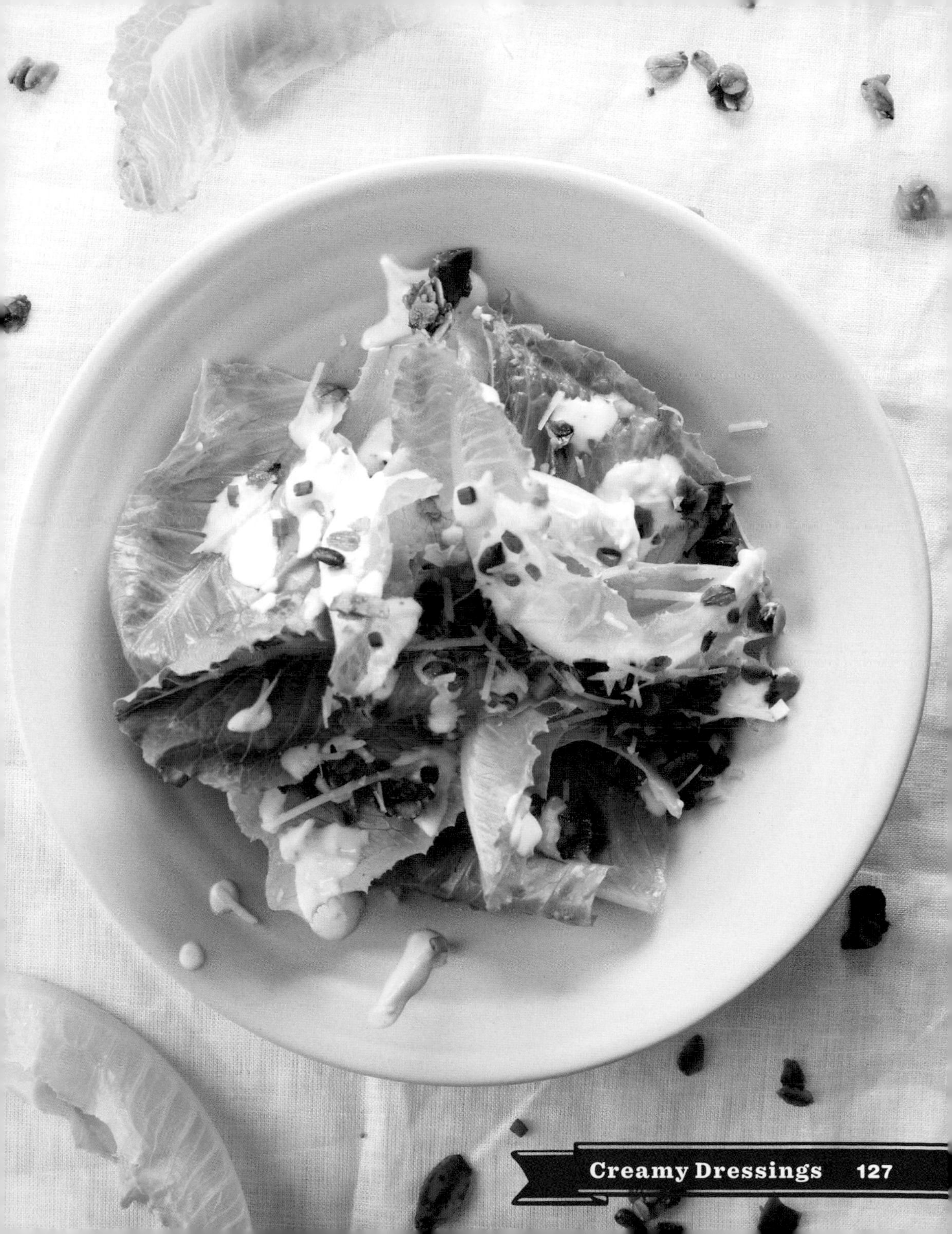

Thousand Island Dressing

If you've ever enjoyed In-N-Out's spread, you're going to like this recipe. Now you can avoid the lines at the fast food joint and just make it yourself—trust me, you won't meet a sandwich this stuff won't improve.

Whisk all ingredients together until they emulsify.

INGREDIENTS

¾ cup mayonnaise

⅓ cup sweet chili sauce

2 tablespoons dill pickles, chopped

2 tablespoons chives, chopped

2 tablespoons pimento, chopped

1 teaspoon capers

2–3 dashes of hot sauce

1 hardboiled egg, chopped

1 tablespoon lemon juice, freshly squeezed

AS WITH THE RANCH, THIS RECIPE OFFERS PLENTY OF OPPORTUNITY FOR EXPERIMENTATION. BELOW ARE A COUPLE EASY VARIATIONS, BUT DEFINITELY TRY COMING UP WITH YOUR OWN FAVORITES!

- LIGHT THOUSAND ISLAND: Replace the mayonnaise with plain Greek yogurt.

- SMOKY THOUSAND ISLAND: Add 1 teaspoon of smoked paprika

Russian Dressing

ACTIVE TIME: 5 MINUTES • TOTAL TIME: 5 MINUTES • SERVING SIZE: 1¼ CUPS

For my money, Russian dressing is best used when spread generously spread on rye bread with turkey, Swiss cheese and fresh coleslaw. New Jersey readers know this as a "Sloppy Joe;" if you're ever out there, find the nearest deli and get one immediately! Feel free to try it with pastrami as well.

INGREDIENTS:

1 tablespoon onion, grated

1 cup mayonnaise

¼ cup ketchup

4 teaspoons horseradish, adjusted to taste

½ teaspoon hot sauce

1 teaspoon Dijon mustard

1 teaspoon Worcestershire sauce

¼ teaspoon sweet paprika

1 teaspoon sea salt

Whisk all the ingredients in bowl until they've emulsified.

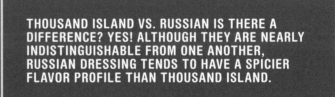

THOUSAND ISLAND VS. RUSSIAN IS THERE A DIFFERENCE? YES! ALTHOUGH THEY ARE NEARLY INDISTINGUISHABLE FROM ONE ANOTHER, RUSSIAN DRESSING TENDS TO HAVE A SPICIER FLAVOR PROFILE THAN THOUSAND ISLAND.

FOR A LIGHT RUSSIAN, REPLACE THE MAYONNAISE WITH PLAIN GREEK YOGURT.

Classic Blue Cheese Dressing

ACTIVE TIME: 5 MINUTES • TOTAL TIME: 5 MINUTES • SERVING SIZE: 1½ CUPS

Blue cheese isn't for everyone, but in a dressing its flavor becomes slightly subdued. This dressing is perfect for spreading over a burger or drizzling over a simple salad at your next barbecue.

Blend the ingredients until smooth, stirring in blue cheese and chopped chives at the end. If the mixture needs to be thinned slightly, add a dash of buttermilk.

INGREDIENTS:

- cup of mayonnaise
- ¼ cup sour cream
- 2 tablespoons lemon juice, freshly squeezed
- 1 teaspoon black pepper, freshly ground
- 1 teaspoon salt
- 1 teaspoon Tabasco
- 1 cup crumbled blue cheese or Stilton
- 2-3 dashes of Tabasco sauce

BECAUSE BLUE CHEESE AND SMOKINESS GO TOGETHER LIKE PB&J, HERE ARE TWO POPULAR VARIATIONS FOR YOU:

- **BACON BLUE CHEESE DRESSING:** Stir in 5 slices of cooked crispy bacon.

- **SMOKY BLUE CHEESE DRESSING:** Add 1 teaspoon of smoked paprika.

Creamy Goat Cheese Dressing

ACTIVE TIME: 10 MINUTES • TOTAL TIME: 10 MINUTES • SERVING SIZE: 1 CUP

¾ cup goat cheese, crumbled

¼ cup tablespoons lemon juice, freshly squeezed

½ cup extra virgin olive oil

1 teaspoon salt

1 teaspoon black pepper, freshly ground

ADD HERBS! FOR GOAT CHEESE–HERB DRESSING, ADD ANY COMBINATION OF TARRAGON, BASIL, PARSLEY, HERBS DE PROVENCE AND OREGANO, TO TASTE.

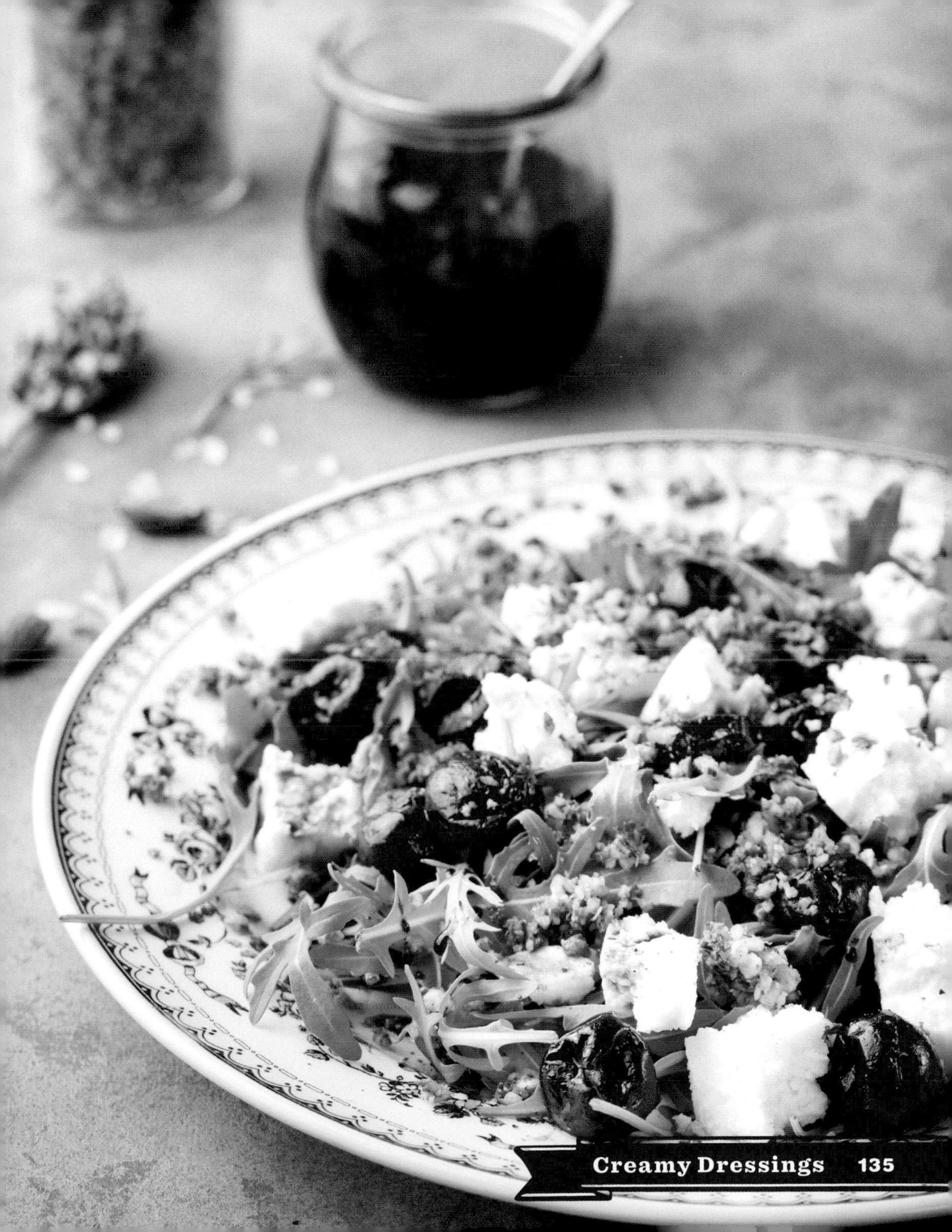

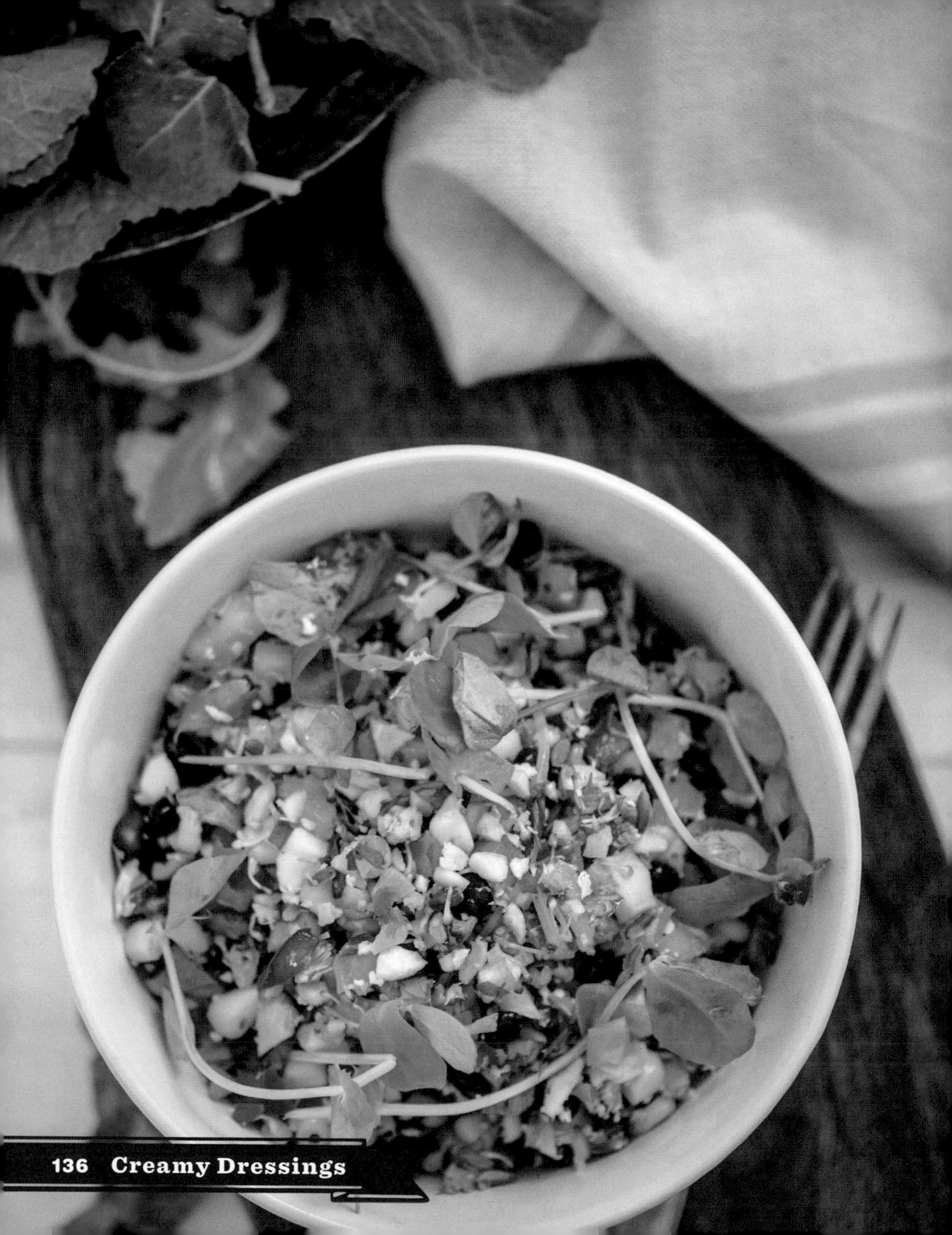

Creamy Chipotle and Adobo Dressing

ACTIVE TIME: 5 MINUTES • TOTAL TIME: 5 MINUTES • SERVING SIZE: ¾ CUP

Perfect for spreading on your favorite veggie burger!

Whisk ingredients in a small bowl until the mixture has emulsified.

INGREDIENTS:

½ cup Greek yogurt

2 chipotles in adobo sauce

1 teaspoon of adobo sauce

½ teaspoon salt

½ teaspoon black pepper, freshly ground

1 teaspoon honey

1 teaspoon Dijon mustard

1 tablespoon lime juice, freshly squeezed

Creamy Harissa Dressing

A chili pepper paste available at most supermarkets today, harissa is a blend of sweet and hot chilis, garlic, coriander, caraway seeds and other spices. This recipe doubles as a great dip for raw veggies or spread for your next burger.

INGREDIENTS:

1 cup plain Greek yogurt

1 teaspoon Indian ...
water or garlic ...

1 ... tablespoon ...
... teaspoon ...

... lemon juice, ...
freshly squeezed

½ teaspoon salt

¼ teaspoon pepper

Whisk all the ingredients in a bowl until evenly mixed.

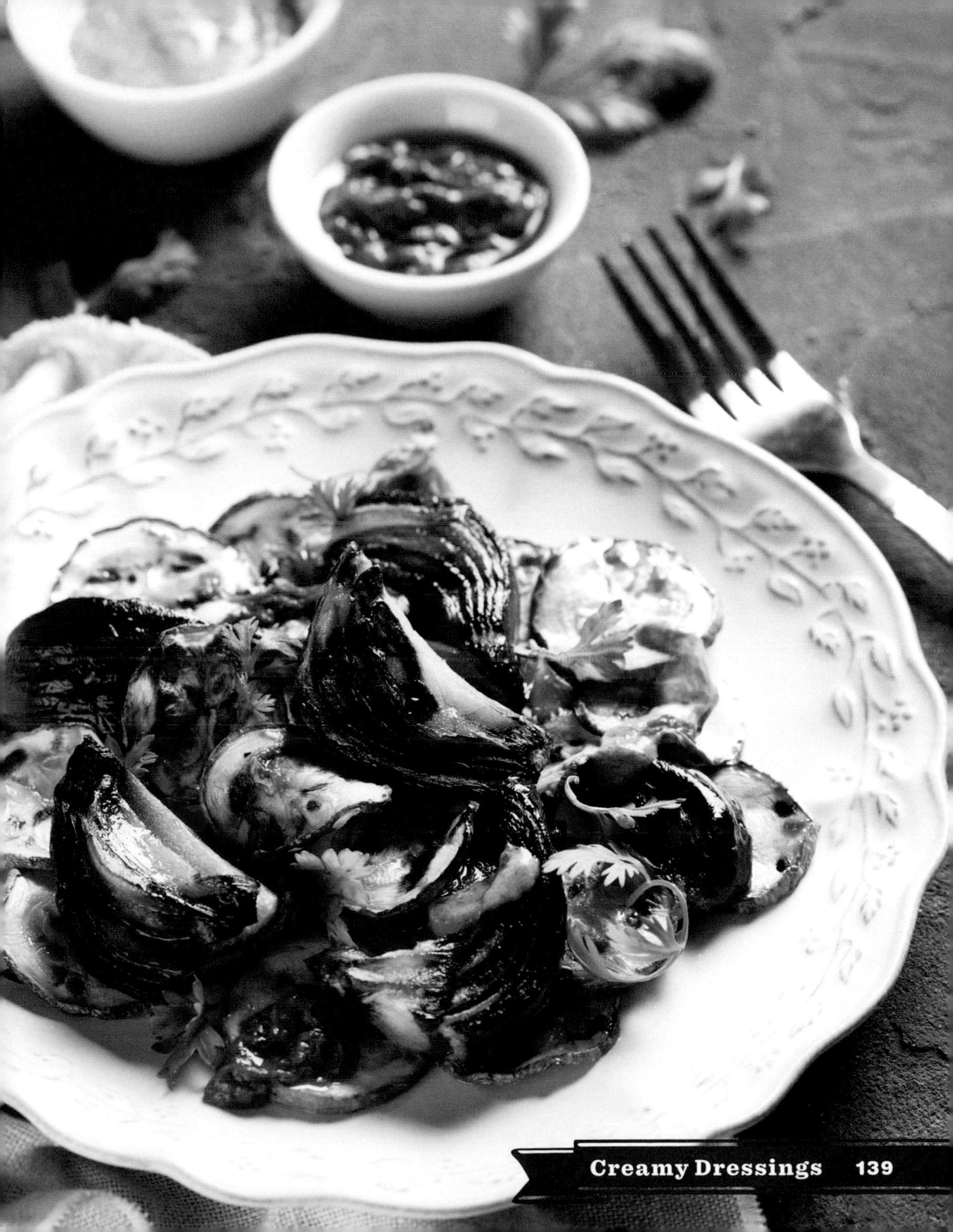

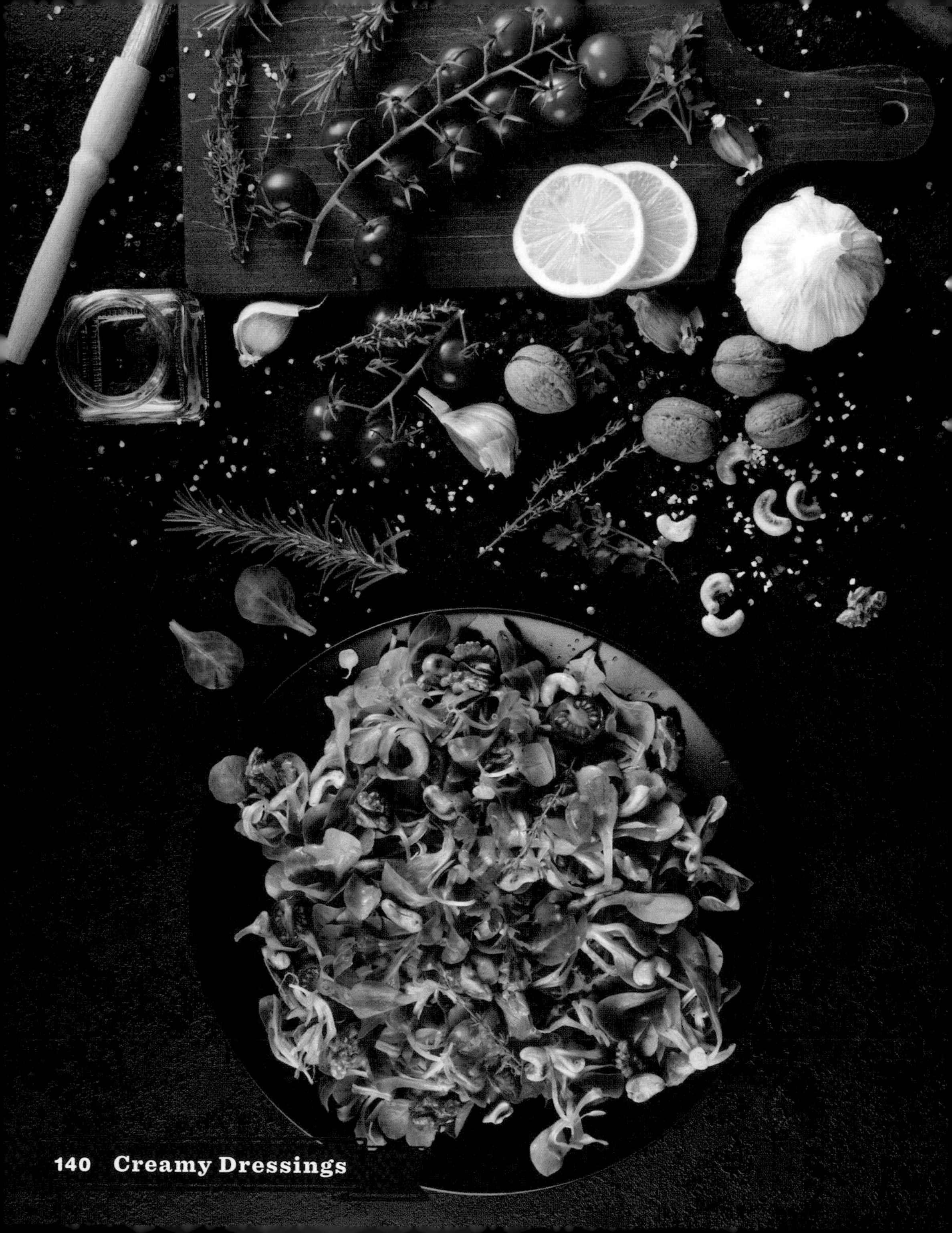

Creamy Horseradish-Mustard Dressing

ACTIVE TIME: 5 MINUTES • TOTAL TIME: 5 MINUTES • SERVING SIZE: ¾ CUP

The sweet flavors of the honey and apple cider vinegar complement the tangy horseradish to create a creamy dressing that pairs perfectly with a sandwich topped with grilled steak.

1. Mix the mayonnaise, vinegar, and mustard together.

2.

INGREDIENTS

1 teaspoon salt

1 teaspoon black pepper, freshly ground

¼ cup mayonnaise

¼ cup apple cider vinegar

2 tablespoons prepared horseradish

2 tablespoons whole-grain mustard

2 teaspoons honey

¼ cup olive oil

Bold Flavors

This section contains all of the most unique recipes I've compiled over the years. Some are regional; some are classics; some are just plain bizarre. I promise, they're all delicious! Next time you see a spice store, take a few extra minutes to walk around and smell some new herbs and spices. You might be surprised by the scents that awaken your senses and inspire you to experiment with your next dressing. This section attempts to translate that feeling into real, bold recipes. Use these with the intention of stealing the show!

Carrot-Ginger Dressing

Fresh ginger root is one of my favorite ingredients to use; it's amazing how much flavor gets packed into such a small root. Any Asian-inspired dish can always benefit from a hint of ginger. Serve this over a chopped romaine, tomato and cucumber salad or use it to marinate grilled chicken.

1 Cook your chopped carrot in boiling water until soft. Remove soft carrots and set aside ½ cup of the cooking water.

2 Blend ingredients until smooth.

INGREDIENTS:

1 chopped carrot, boiled until soft

½ cup cooking water

2 tablespoons rice vinegar

2 tablespoons peeled ginger, chopped

1 teaspoon sugar

1 teaspoon soy sauce

1 teaspoon sesame oil

1 teaspoon salt

1 teaspoon pepper

Asian Sesame Dressing

Perfect for an Asian chicken salad or just grilled chicken over a light spring mix, this light and refreshing dressing is great to have in your back pocket.

INGREDIENTS:

2 tablespoons cider vinegar

1 tablespoon brown sugar

1½ teaspoons peeled ginger, grated

3 tablespoons sesame oil

⅓ cup vegetable oil

½ teaspoon salt

½ teaspoon black pepper, freshly ground

1 teaspoon sesame seeds, white or black

Whisk the ingredients in a small bowl or shake them in a jar and serve.

Miso-Ginger Dressing

ACTIVE TIME: 10 MINUTES • TOTAL TIME: 10 MINUTES • SERVING SIZE: ¾ CUP

Miso is a traditional Japanese ingredient that has been used for centuries. It is high in protein, vitamins and minerals, making it a trendy option in today's more health-conscious world. Made from fermented soybeans, miso is salty, savory, earthy and a little sweet.

Add ingredients to a blender and blend until smooth.

INGREDIENTS:

1 tablespoon miso paste

1 tablespoon peeled ginger, grated

¼ cup lime juice, freshly squeezed

½ garlic clove

1 chopped scallion

1 teaspoon Sriracha

½ teaspoon sugar

½ cup vegetable oil

Avocado-Wasabi

Avocado has become such a versatile ingredient. Blend this together with or without the wasabi paste and serve over your favorite spring vegetables—in my case, asparagus, snap peas and radishes!

INGREDIENTS:

½ ripe avocado, pureed

1½ teaspoons wasabi paste

3 tablespoons each rice vinegar

3 tablespoons water

½ teaspoon salt

¼ cup vegetable oil

Add ingredients to a blender and blend until smooth.

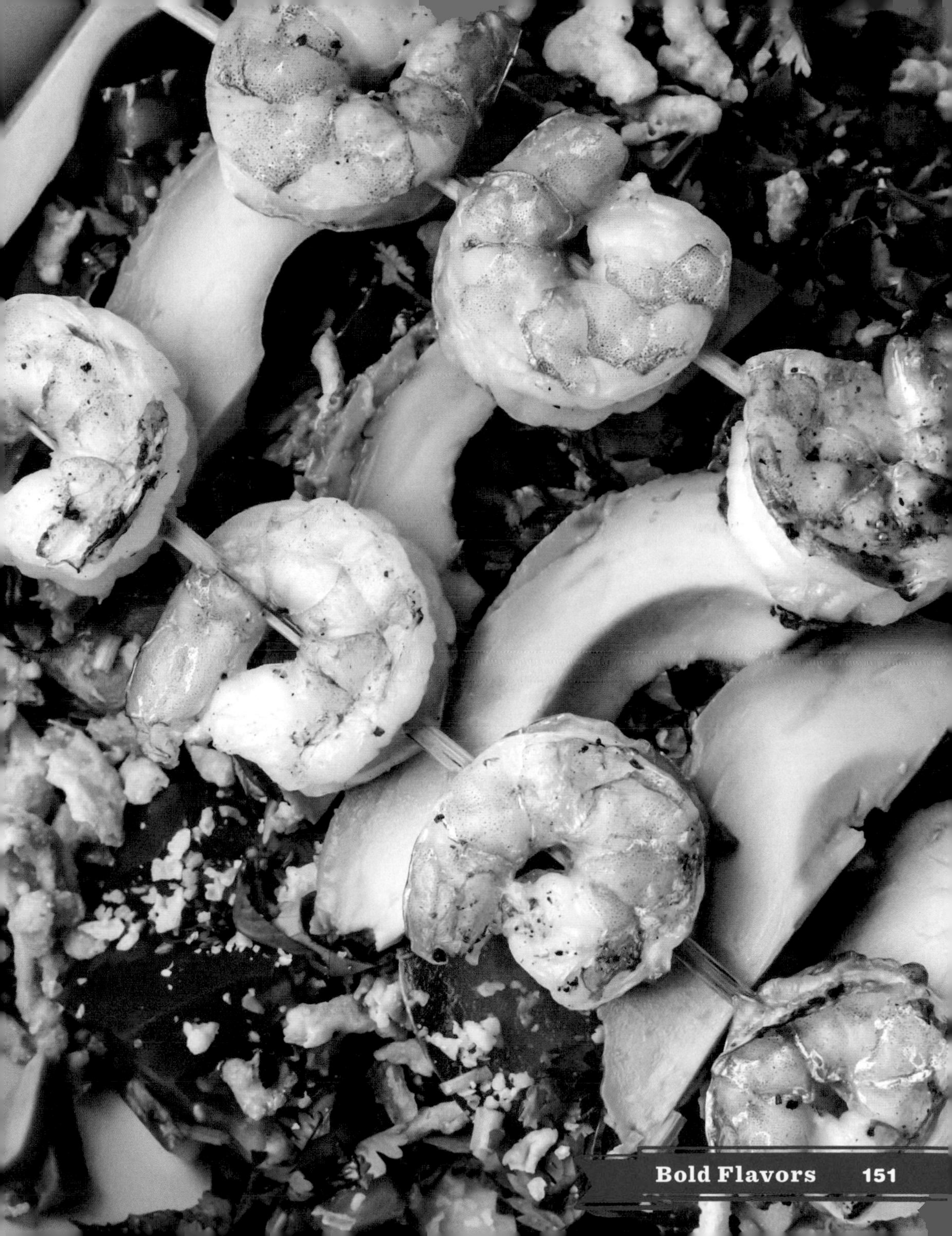

Spicy Thai Dressing

This is a great dipping sauce for any vegetable (raw or cooked!) or your favorite kind of dumpling.

INGREDIENTS:

¼ cup lime juice

1 tablespoon fish sauce

1 teaspoon sugar

½ teaspoon Sriracha

¼ teaspoon salt

¼ cup vegetable oil

Whisk ingredients in a small bowl until evenly mixed.

Peanut-Lime Dressing

ACTIVE TIME: 10 MINUTES • TOTAL TIME: 10 MINUTES • SERVING SIZE: ¾ CUP

Perfect for a Pad Thai–inspired noodle salad, hot or cold, or as a vegetable dipping sauce!

Add ingredients to a blender and blend until smooth.

INGREDIENTS:

¼ cup creamy peanut butter

3 tablespoons water

2 tablespoons lime juice, freshly squeezed

1 tablespoon rice vinegar

1 tablespoon peeled ginger, chopped

2 teaspoons soy sauce

2 teaspoons honey

Chili-Soy Dressing

This dressing's delicate flavor balance doubles as a perfect noodle dressing and also a wonderful marinade for grilled salmon.

INGREDIENTS:

¼ cup sugar

3 tablespoons soy sauce

1 green or red Thai chili, finely chopped

1½ inches ginger root, peeled and minced

1 clove garlic, minced

2 tablespoons dark soy sauce

2 tablespoons mushroom soy sauce

2 tablespoons rice wine vinegar

1 teaspoon black pepper, freshly ground

1 Cook sugar and soy sauce in a small saucepan over medium heat until dissolved, stirring often.

2 Once cooled, whisk in all ingredients thoroughly.

Anchovy-Miso Dressing

This dressing is perfect for salty food–lovers. The cilantro and the lemon zest add fresh flavors that brighten this dressing right up.

1 Combine anchovies, lemon zest, lemon juice, vinegar, soy sauce, miso and sugar in a bowl. Whisk the oil in slowly.

2 Once you've added the oil, add the scallions, chili, cilantro and celery leaves.

INGREDIENTS:

4 oil-packed anchovy filets

1 teaspoon lemon zest

2 tablespoons lemon juice, freshly squeezed

2 tablespoons rice wine vinegar

1 tablespoon low-sodium soy sauce

4 teaspoons white miso

¼ teaspoon sugar

1 tablespoon vegetable oil

½ cup celery leaves

2 scallions, finely chopped

1 cup cilantro, finely chopped

1 serrano chili, minced

2 teaspoons black sesame seeds

1 teaspoon salt

1 teaspoon black pepper, freshly ground

Ginger-Mezcal Dressing

ACTIVE TIME: 10 MINUTES • **TOTAL TIME: 10 MINUTES** • **SERVING SIZE: ¾ CUP**

Mezcal is on trend these days, so it helps to find creative ways to use it. Smoky mezcal and lime juice are a perfect match in any situation.

INGREDIENTS:

2 teaspoons ginger, thinly sliced

3 tablespoons lime juice, freshly squeezed

¼ cucumber, diced

2 tablespoons mezcal

½ teaspoon agave nectar

1 jalapeño, thinly sliced

2 tablespoons of steeped chamomile tea

1 teaspoon salt

½ cup olive oil

Whisk ingredients in a small bowl until the mixture has emulsified.

Lychee Ginger Dressing

The lychee fruit's sweet, floral fragrance is so unique. I like to use this on dark green salads, like kale with sliced almonds and fresh orange slices.

Whisk the ingredients in a small bowl until the mixture has emulsified.

INGREDIENTS:

½ cup grape seed oil

⅓ cup rice wine vinegar

2 tablespoons lychee juice

3 tablespoons fresh ginger, minced

2 teaspoons soy sauce

2 teaspoons agave

2 teaspoons lemon juice

1 teaspoon orange zest

½ teaspoon salt

¼ teaspoon black pepper, freshly ground

Sunflower Seed Dressing

ACTIVE TIME: 15 MINUTES • TOTAL TIME: 15 MINUTES • SERVING SIZE: ¾ CUP

Sunflower seeds aren't just for the baseball field! Try them in this nutty blend and drizzle over roasted acorn or butternut squash.

INGREDIENTS:

1 tablespoon sunflower seeds, toasted

½ cup basil leaves

1 tablespoon lime juice, freshly squeezed

¼ teaspoon honey

¼ teaspoon salt

½ cup olive oil

1 Toast the sunflower seeds in a dry skillet until they've lightly browned.

2 Put all the ingredients in a blender and blend until smooth.

Green Curry Dressing

This Thai favorite is incredibly flexible—use it over rice, noodles, vegetables or any meat and enjoy its sweet and complex flavors.

Whisk the ingredients in a small bowl until the mixture has emulsified.

INGREDIENTS:

¾ cup coconut milk

1 tablespoon green Thai curry paste

1 tablespoon sugar

2 packed tablespoon cilantro, finely chopped

Lime juice squeezed from ½ lime

¾ cup peanut oil

Red Curry Dressing

Everybody has a favorite Thai curry, and every Thai restaurant offers a wide variety of them, but green and red are the two you can always count on seeing. The fish sauce in this recipe gives it the slight edge in my mind, but see for yourself!

INGREDIENTS:

1 cup coconut milk

½ cup chicken broth

2 tablespoons peanut butter

2 tablespoons red curry paste

1½ tablespoons fish sauce

Lime juice squeezed from ½ lime

3 tablespoons brown sugar

⅓ cup peanuts, crushed

Whisk the ingredients in a small bowl until the mixture has emulsified.

Green Goddess Dressing

This is a classic dressing named, of course, for its beautiful green hue. The vibrant green literally shows how flavorful and herbaceous this dressing is!

INGREDIENTS:

2 cups watercress

4 anchovy fillets packed in oil, drained

½ cup mayonnaise

2 tablespoons sour cream

½ cup flat-leaf parsley leaves

2 tablespoons fresh chives, chopped

2 tablespoons fresh tarragon, chopped

1½ tablespoons white wine vinegar

1 teaspoon salt

1 teaspoon black pepper, freshly ground

Blend all the ingredients until smooth.

IF YOU WANT TO MAKE YOUR GREEN GODDESS *EVEN HEALTHIER*, TRY THESE TWO VARIATIONS:

- AVOCADO GREEN GODDESS DRESSING: Replace mayonnaise with 1 avocado.

- HEALTHY GREEN GODDESS DRESSING: Replace mayonnaise with nonfat Greek yogurt.

Buttermilk Green Goddess Dressing

ACTIVE TIME: 10 MINUTES • TOTAL TIME: 10 MINUTES • SERVING SIZE: ¾ CUP

Using buttermilk in this variation adds some extra tang to an already flavorful salad topper.

Blend all the ingredients until smooth.

CILANTRO-LIME GREEN GODDESS

REPLACE THE MAYONNAISE WITH ONE AVOCADO AND ¼ CUP OF COCONUT CREAM.

- REPLACE THE TARRAGON WITH CILANTRO.
- REPLACE THE LEMON JUICE WITH LIME JUICE.

INGREDIENTS:

½ cup mayonnaise

⅓ cup buttermilk

¼ cup fresh chives, chopped

¼ cup flat-leaf parsley, coarsely chopped

1 tablespoon fresh tarragon, chopped

1 tablespoon fresh lemon juice

2 anchovy fillets packed in oil, drained and chopped

1 clove garlic, chopped

Kosher salt and black pepper, freshly ground

Grilled Corn Dressing

ACTIVE TIME: 20 MINUTES • TOTAL TIME: 20 MINUTES • SERVING SIZE: ¾ CUP

This summery dressing needn't be kept away until Memorial Day—just use frozen corn to enjoy this sweet, rich dressing all year long.

INGREDIENTS:

1 grilled cob of corn, or 1 cup frozen corn kernels, sautéed

Corn water from the cob, if applicable

2 teaspoons salt

1 teaspoon black pepper

½ cup olive oil

1 teaspoon paprika

3 tablespoons white wine vinegar

1 Grill or sauté your corn and remove the kernels if necessary.

2 Using the back of a knife, scrape the bare cob to gather the leftover water and add it to your blender. If you didn't use corn on the cob, you can skip this step.

3 Place all your ingredients in a blender and blend until smooth.

Pesto Potato Salad Dressing

ACTIVE TIME: 10 MINUTES • TOTAL TIME: 10 MINUTES • SERVING SIZE: ¾ CUP

Turn up to volume on regular potato salad. This is my favorite side to bring to a BBQ.

1 In a food processor, combine the basil, pine nuts, salt, pepper, lemon juice and lemon zest into a coarse chop. Slowly drizzle in the olive oil until mixture becomes a fine paste.

2 Stir in the Parmesan cheese and diced bell pepper. Toss on cooked and marinated potatoes and serve.

IF PINE NUTS AREN'T YOUR THING, ALMONDS AND WALNUTS MAKE TASTY ALTERNATIVES. ALSO, YOU CAN ADD 1 CUP OF KALE FOR A HEARTIER PESTO!

INGREDIENTS:

1½ cup fresh basil leaves

⅔ cup extra virgin olive oil

½ cup pine nuts

2 teaspoons sea salt

2 teaspoons black pepper, freshly ground

¼ cup lemon juice, freshly squeezed

½ cup Parmesan cheese, grated

1 red bell pepper, diced

Roasted Scallion and Feta Dressing

ACTIVE TIME: 10 MINUTES • TOTAL TIME: 10 MINUTES • SERVING SIZE: ¾ CUP

Here's another flavorful dressing that doubles as a dip for crudité or pita chips.

INGREDIENTS:

10 scallions, roasted and chopped

½ cup extra virgin olive oil

¼ teaspoon salt

1 teaspoon black pepper, freshly ground

¾ cup of feta cheese, crumbled

3 tablespoons whole milk, adjusting for desired consistency

2 tablespoons lemon juice, freshly squeezed

1 Preheat your oven to 400 degrees Fahrenheit. Roast your chopped scallions in olive oil, salt and pepper for 20–25 minutes.

2 Crumble the feta cheese and add all ingredients in blender. Blend until smooth.

Feta-Oregano Dressing

ACTIVE TIME: 10 MINUTES • TOTAL TIME: 10 MINUTES • SERVING SIZE: ¾ CUP

These classic Greek flavors are delicious in any context. Try this over a salad or spread it over a lamb burger!

INGREDIENTS:

- ¾ cup feta cheese
- 2 tablespoons oregano
- ½ cup extra virgin olive oil
- ¼ cup lemon juice, freshly squeezed
- 1 teaspoon of black pepper
- 1 teaspoon of salt

Whisk ingredients in a small bowl until the mixture has emulsified. Use water to adjust the consistency to your liking.

Spicy Arugula Dressing

ACTIVE TIME: 10 MINUTES • TOTAL TIME: 10 MINUTES • SERVING SIZE: ¾ CUP

Toss with cooked penne, fusilli, or angel hair pasta for a quick and satisfying dinner.

Purée the chili, arugula, mint, vegetable oil, olive oil, lime zest, lime juice and sugar in a blender until smooth. Season with salt and pepper.

INGREDIENTS:

1 serrano chile or jalapeño, chopped and deseeded (optional)

½ cup arugula

½ cup mint leaves

½ cup vegetable oil

¼ cup olive oil

½ teaspoon lime zest, finely grated

¼ cup lime juice

½ teaspoon sugar

1teaspoon salt

1 teaspoon black pepper, freshly ground

Grated Tomato Dressing

Mediterranean simplicity! Use the summer tomato bounty in this vinaigrette to top crostini, pasta or greens.

INGREDIENTS:

½ cup extra virgin olive oil

2 tomatoes, grated

1 clove garlic, grated

1 teaspoon black pepper, freshly ground

1 teaspoon salt

½ teaspoon dried oregano

Whisk ingredients in a small bowl or shake them in a jar and serve.

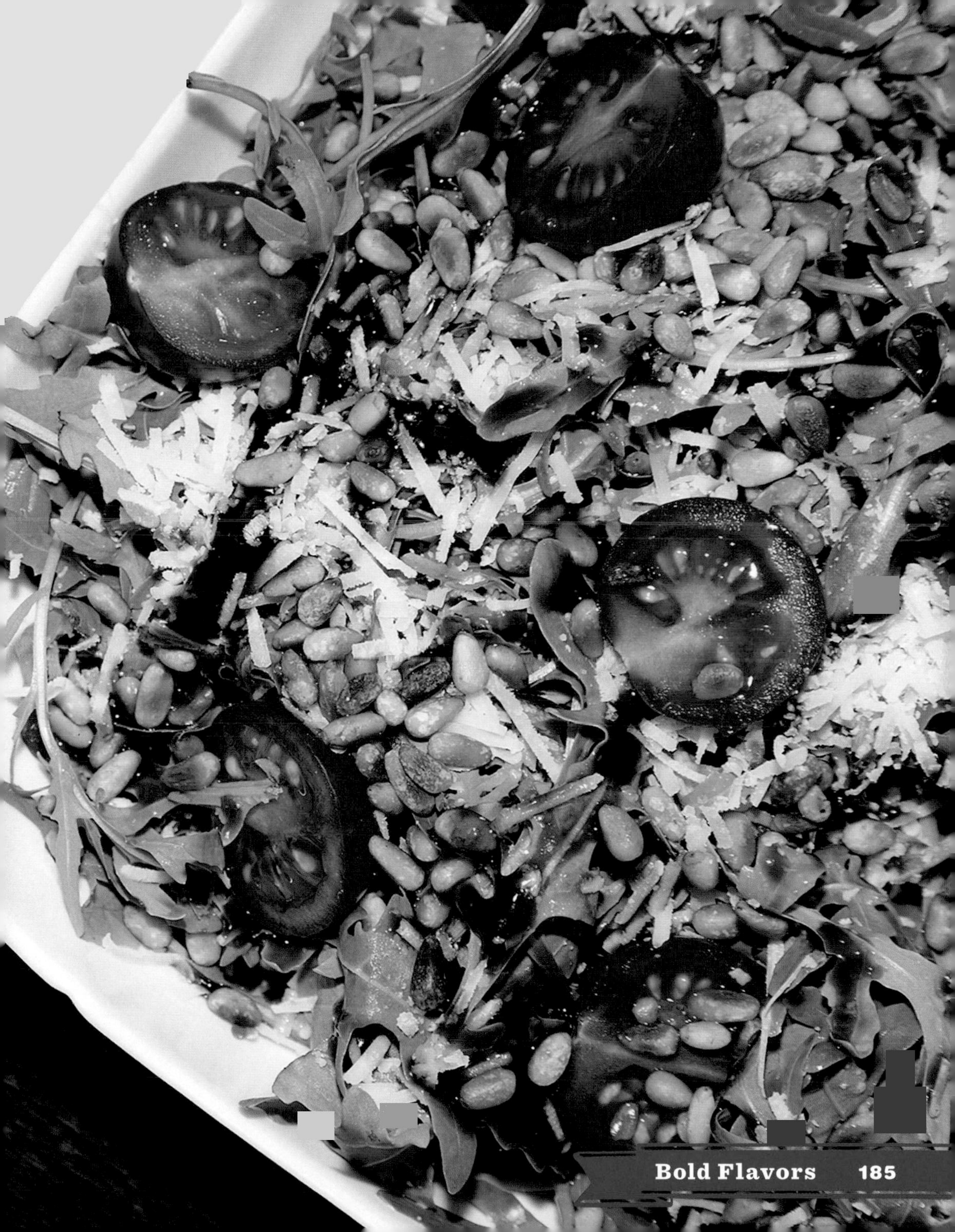

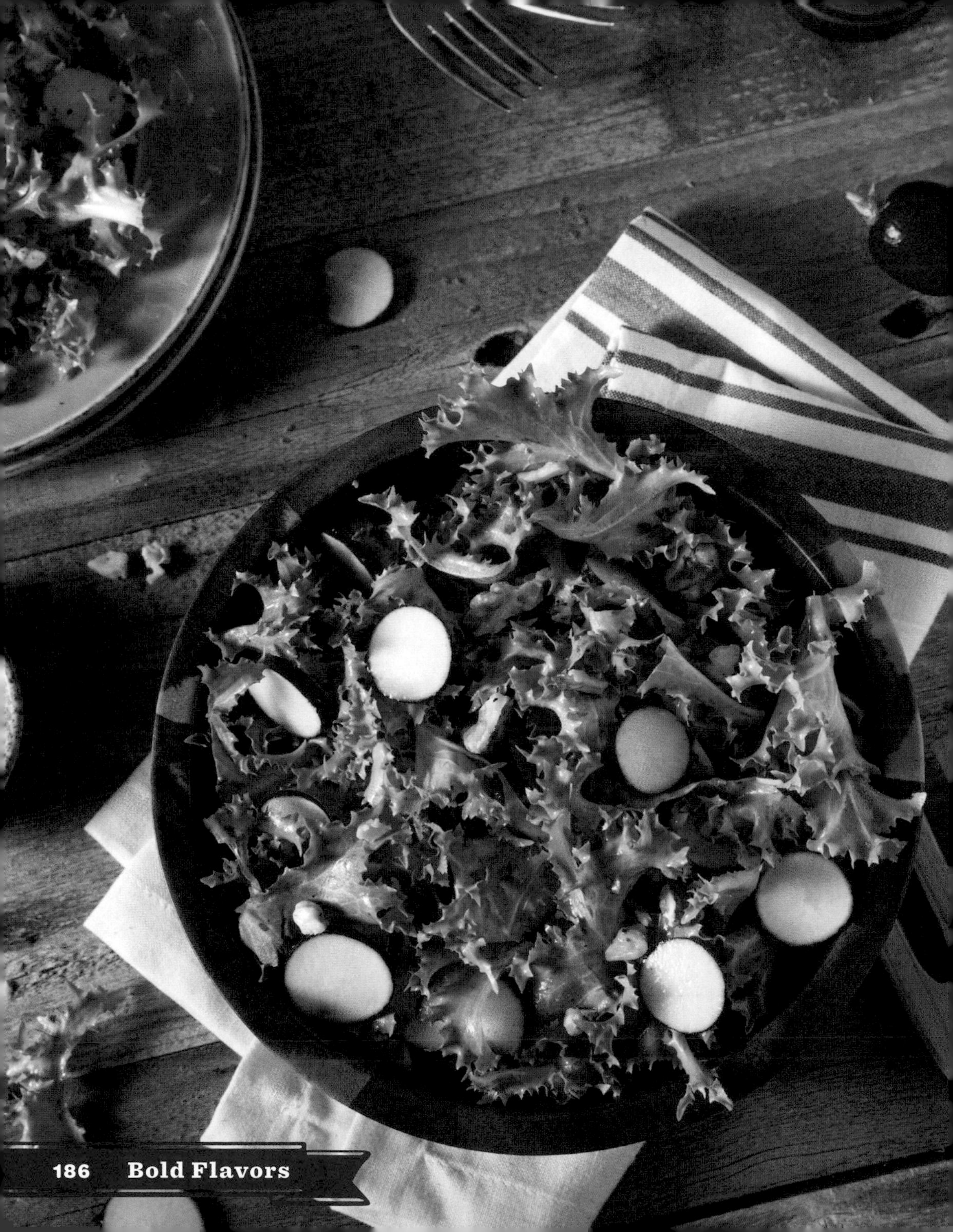

Spicy Honey Mustard Dressing

Spicy, savory and sweet, this dressing is nothing if not versatile; it can be tossed with sliced chicken, greens, fried zucchini or anything else you feel like trying. Have fun experimenting with different mustards and honeys to put your own spin on it!

Whisk ingredients in a small bowl or shake them in a jar and serve.

REPLACE THE DIJON WITH GRAINY MUSTARD FOR ADDED TEXTURE AND A SHARPER FLAVOR!

INGREDIENTS:

2 teaspoons honey

2 teaspoons Dijon mustard

½ cup of vegetable oil

2½ tablespoons lime juice, freshly squeezed

Zest of ½ lime

1 teaspoon salt

2 teaspoons fresh lemon thyme

1 jalapeño, finely chopped, to taste.

Pinch of black pepper, freshly ground

Mint Crema

Serve alongside roasted or grilled lamb. Mint and lamb is a timeless combination!

INGREDIENTS:

2 tablespoons pumpkin seeds, toasted

1 cup mint leaves

½ cup olive oil

1 tablespoon honey

1 teaspoon lime juice, freshly squeezed

½ cup water

⅓ cup sour cream

1 teaspoon salt

1 Toast your pumpkin seeds in a dry skillet until very lightly browned.

2 Place all ingredients in a blender and blend until the mixture is smooth.

Bold Flavors

Salsa Verde Dressing

Perfect over grilled steak, chicken or pork, as well as any grilled vegetables!

Combine all ingredients in a food processor until they form a paste.

INGREDIENTS:

1 cup Italian parsley

½ cup cilantro

1 teaspoon shallot, minced

1anchovy filet, minced

1 tablespoon capers

1 clove garlic

1 tablespoon red wine vinegar

½ cup extra virgin olive oil

Chipotle-Mezcal Dressing

ACTIVE TIME: 10 MINUTES • TOTAL TIME: 10 MINUTES • SERVING SIZE: ¾ CUP

Next time you're serving margaritas, be sure to whip this dressing up and watch the salad disappear from the bowl. This also makes a great spread on sandwiches or tortillas!

INGREDIENTS:

¼ cup chipotle in adobo, including 1 whole chipotle

2 tablespoons lime juice, freshly squeezed

3 tablespoons white wine vinegar

½ cup grape seed oil

2 tablespoons mezcal

⅓ cup water

1 teaspoon salt

1 teaspoon black pepper, freshly ground

Blend all of the ingredients until the mixture is smooth.

Avocado-Habanero Crema

ACTIVE TIME: 15 MINUTES • **TOTAL TIME:** 15 MINUTES • **SERVING SIZE:** 1¼ CUP

This recipe packs quite a punch with its touch of habanero, but the avocado and sour cream quickly cool down that chili heat.

Combine all the ingredients in a blender and blend until smooth.

INGREDIENTS:

1 avocado, pitted and scooped

½ habanero, seeded

1 cup sour cream

¼ cup olive oil

½ teaspoon honey

1 teaspoon salt

1 teaspoon black pepper, freshly ground

Chili-Mango Dressing

ACTIVE TIME: 5 MINUTES • TOTAL TIME: 5 MINUTES • SERVING SIZE: ¾ CUP

This dressing is inspired by some time I spent in Guatemala. I was served an unripe mango dusted with a salt and chili powder mixture—it sounds odd, but I still can't get its flavor out of my head. Try this over chicken or pork tacos.

INGREDIENTS:

1 fresh mango, peeled

1 teaspoon chili powder

¼ cup canola or grape seed oil

1 teaspoon salt

1 teaspoon black pepper, freshly ground

3 tablespoons rice wine vinegar

Blend all of the ingredients until the mixture is smooth.

Lime and Honey Dressing

ACTIVE TIME: 5 MINUTES • **TOTAL TIME: 5 MINUTES** • **SERVING SIZE: 1 CUP**

These fresh, light flavors can highlight a salad or marinate your favorite fish.

Whisk ingredients in a small bowl until the mixture has emulsified.

INGREDIENTS:

¼ cup lime juice, freshly squeezed

¾ cup extra virgin olive oil

2 tablespoons honey

1 teaspoon salt

Coriander Dressing

ACTIVE TIME: 10 MINUTES • TOTAL TIME: 10 MINUTES • SERVING SIZE: ¾ CUP

This dynamic dressing is particularly good over any Mexican entrée, but I still encourage you to drizzle it over any mixed salad. I especially love how its complex flavors, drawing from Asia and South America, can mask the fact that I'm using premade salad mix!

INGREDIENTS:

1 tablespoon coriander seeds, toasted

¼ cup cilantro

1 clove garlic, roasted

½ small shallot, minced

1 teaspoon honey

½ cup extra virgin olive oil

3 tablespoons lime juice

½ teaspoon salt

1 teaspoon black pepper, freshly ground

1 In a dry skillet, toast your coriander seeds until slightly browned. Remove from heat and ground into a fine powder.

2 Whisk the ingredients in a small bowl until the mixture has emulsified.

Pink Peppercorn Dressing

Not an actual peppercorn, these dried fruits from the cashew family are named for their amazing resemblance to the pepper we know and love. Still, these little fruits have a peppery kick which, combined with their with floral undertones, make them ideal for dressing a bed of lettuce topped with grilled tofu or steak.

Whisk the ingredients in a small bowl until the mixture has emulsified.

INGREDIENTS:

2 tablespoons of pink peppercorns, very coarsely crushed (mortar and pestle is best tool)

½ cup grape seed oil

1 teaspoon salt

3 tablespoons red wine vinegar

Roasted Beet Purée Dressing

ACTIVE TIME: 10 MINUTES • TOTAL TIME: 10 MINUTES • SERVING SIZE: 1 CUP

Toss on kale with sliced almonds and goat cheese.

INGREDIENTS:

2 cups beets, finely chopped

2 tablespoons apple cider vinegar

½ teaspoon salt

2 tablespoons water

2 tablespoons grape seed oil

Puree all the ingredients in a blender.

Roasted Fennel Dressing

With its bold anise flavor, fennel isn't for everyone. But it *is* incredibly good for you, and can elevate any salad when utilized correctly. This dressing tries to play off of fennel's flavor rather than simply amplify it.

1. Preheat the oven to 400 degrees Fahrenheit. Toss the sliced fennel with 1 tablespoon of olive oil, spread it on a sheet pan and roast for 20 minutes, or until golden brown.

2. When your fennel has cooled, place all the ingredients in blender and blend until smooth.

INGREDIENTS:

2 fennel bulbs, cored and thinly sliced

½ cup low-sodium chicken broth

3 tablespoons extra virgin olive oil

1 teaspoon salt

1 teaspoon black pepper, freshly ground

3 tablespoons red wine vinegar

2 tablespoons unsalted butter, melted

½ teaspoon Dijon mustard

½ bunch chives, chopped (about ¼ cup)

Butternut Squash Dressing

ACTIVE TIME: 20 MINUTES • TOTAL TIME: 20 MINUTES • SERVING SIZE: ¾ CUP

Drizzle this over kale and homemade sourdough croutons. Add some shaved Parmesan on top and serve.

INGREDIENTS:

1 cup cooked butternut squash

1½ tablespoons olive oil

2 tablespoons water

½ teaspoon cinnamon

¼ teaspoon cumin

1 tablespoon agave nectar

1 teaspoon thyme

1 Cook your butternut squash using your favorite method. For an easy way, bake your sliced squash coated in water and a pinch of salt on 375 degrees Fahrenheit for 45 minutes. When the squash is tender and easily pierced by a fork, remove it.

2 Place all ingredients in a blender and blend until smooth.

> TIP: ADD THREE LEAVES OF MINCED SAGE!

Grapefruit-Papaya Dressing

ACTIVE TIME: 5 MINUTES • **TOTAL TIME: 5 MINUTES** • **SERVING SIZE: ¾ CUP**

Sweet and citrus flavors are perfect with dark bitter greens like kale or mustard greens.

Add all the ingredients in a blender and blend until the mixture is smooth.

INGREDIENTS:

½ papaya, seeded, peeled and diced

½ cup grapefruit juice, freshly squeezed

¼ cup honey

¼ cup water

1 teaspoon salt

Rose Water Dressing

Rose water (or any flower water) is made by steeping petals in water to extract their essential oils. The flavor can be a bit potent, but it's something different to try on your next salad. Try experimenting with different steeping times to get the flavor exactly how you like it.

1 Place ¹/₂ cup of rose petals in a bowl, then pour in 1 cup of boiling water. Allow the rose petals to steep for 20 minutes or so. Strain the bowl and set the water aside.

2 Using ¹/₂ teaspoon of your rose water, whisk all the ingredients in a small bowl until the mixture has emulsified. You can save the rest of the rose water for another cooking endeavor, or add more to your vinaigrette!

INGREDIENTS:

3 tablespoons lemon juice, freshly squeezed

Zest of ½ lemon

½ cup extra virgin olive oil

½ teaspoon rose water

½ teaspoon sea salt

½ teaspoon black pepper, freshly ground

1 teaspoon honey

IF THE ROSE WATER ISN'T TO YOUR LIKING, TRY REPLACING IT WITH ELDER FLOWER WATER OR ORANGE BLOSSOM WATER.

Apricot–Rose Water Dressing

This fruity delight is great on top of dark bitter greens with walnuts, sliced chicken and crumbled goat cheese.

INGREDIENTS:

2 tablespoons apricot preserves

⅓ cup grape seed oil

1½ tablespoons champagne vinegar

1 tablespoon lemon juice, freshly squeezed

½ tablespoon rose water

1/8 teaspoon salt

1 Place ½ cup of rose petals in a bowl, then pour in 1 cup of boiling water. Allow the rose petals to steep for 20 minutes or so. Strain the bowl and set the water aside.

2 Using ½ teaspoon of your rose water, whisk all the ingredients in a small bowl until the mixture has emulsified. You can save the rest of the rose water for later or add more to your vinaigrette!

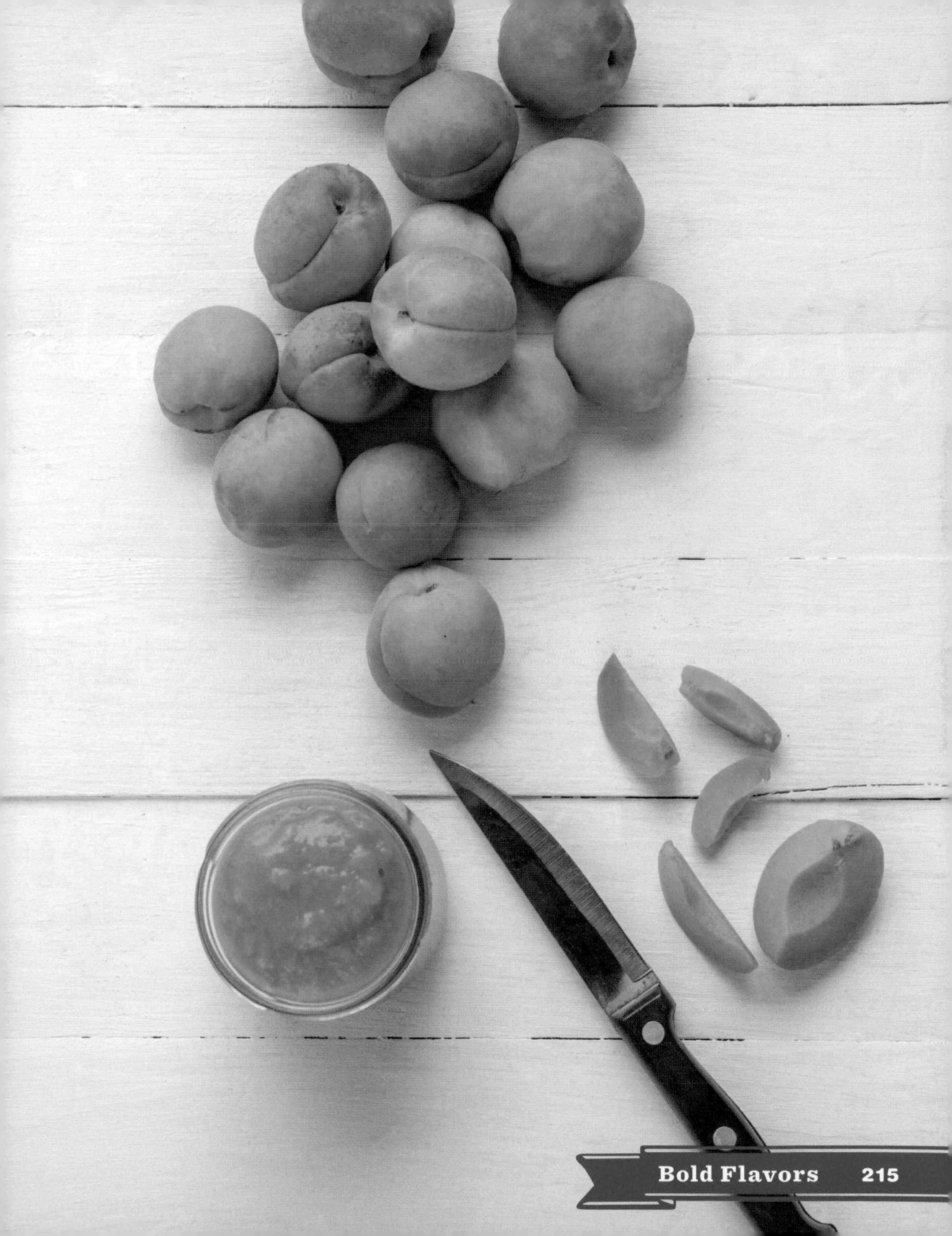

Sauces and Dips

I love hosting dinners and cocktail parties but I always stress about what to serve as appetizers. These options are easy crowd-pleasers that are sure to get your party off to a great start. You've probably figured this out by now, but I believe sauce is the most important part of any dish. The most memorable meals I've had in my life have come with extraordinary sauces. And while I absolutely place dressings under that umbrella, I still couldn't resist dedicating an entire section to sauces and dips. Don't forget, these work just as well with salads as they do with finger foods.

Classic Hollandaise

ACTIVE TIME: 15 MINUTES • TOTAL TIME: 15 MINUTES • SERVING SIZE: 1 CUP

So many cooks don't ever think to make eggs Benedict at home, and I can understand why—it feels like such a brunch treat, doesn't it? But after learning your own Hollandaise recipe, you're going to kick yourself for not doing it sooner! The beauty of this recipe is its simplicity. Some sauces too buttery for you? Not lemony enough? This ensures you'll be able to make yours exactly how you like it.

INGREDIENTS:

1¼ cups (2½ sticks) unsalted butter, cubed

2 large egg yolks

2 tablespoons fresh lemon juice, adjusting to taste

1 teaspoon salt

1 teaspoon black pepper, freshly ground

1 Fill a blender with hot water and set aside. Melt your butter in a small saucepan over medium heat, remove and drain your blender, drying well.

2 Put egg yolks and 2 tablespoons of lemon juice in the blender, cover and blend to combine. While the blender runs, remove its lid insert and slowly pour hot butter in a thin stream, discarding the milk solids at bottom of the saucepan. Blend until creamy sauce forms.

3 Season to taste with salt and pepper, and add lemon juice to taste. Serve immediately.

Vegan Hollandaise

ACTIVE TIME: 5 MINUTES • TOTAL TIME: 5 MINUTES • SERVING SIZE: 1 CUP

It's 2017—vegan eggs Benedict are super easy to make (and shop for)! And they deserve a Hollandaise to match. Try this one out and never look back.

INGREDIENTS:

¾ cup cashew butter

2 teaspoons Dijon mustard

Zest of 1 lemon

¼ cup lemon juice

1 teaspoon garlic powder

½ teaspoon ground turmeric

⅛ teaspoon cayenne pepper

½ cup warm water

1 Combine cashew butter, mustard, lemon zest, lemon juice, garlic powder, turmeric, cayenne and ½ cup of warm water in a blender and blend until smooth. This should take about 1 minute.

2 Add more warm water as needed to reach the desired consistency.

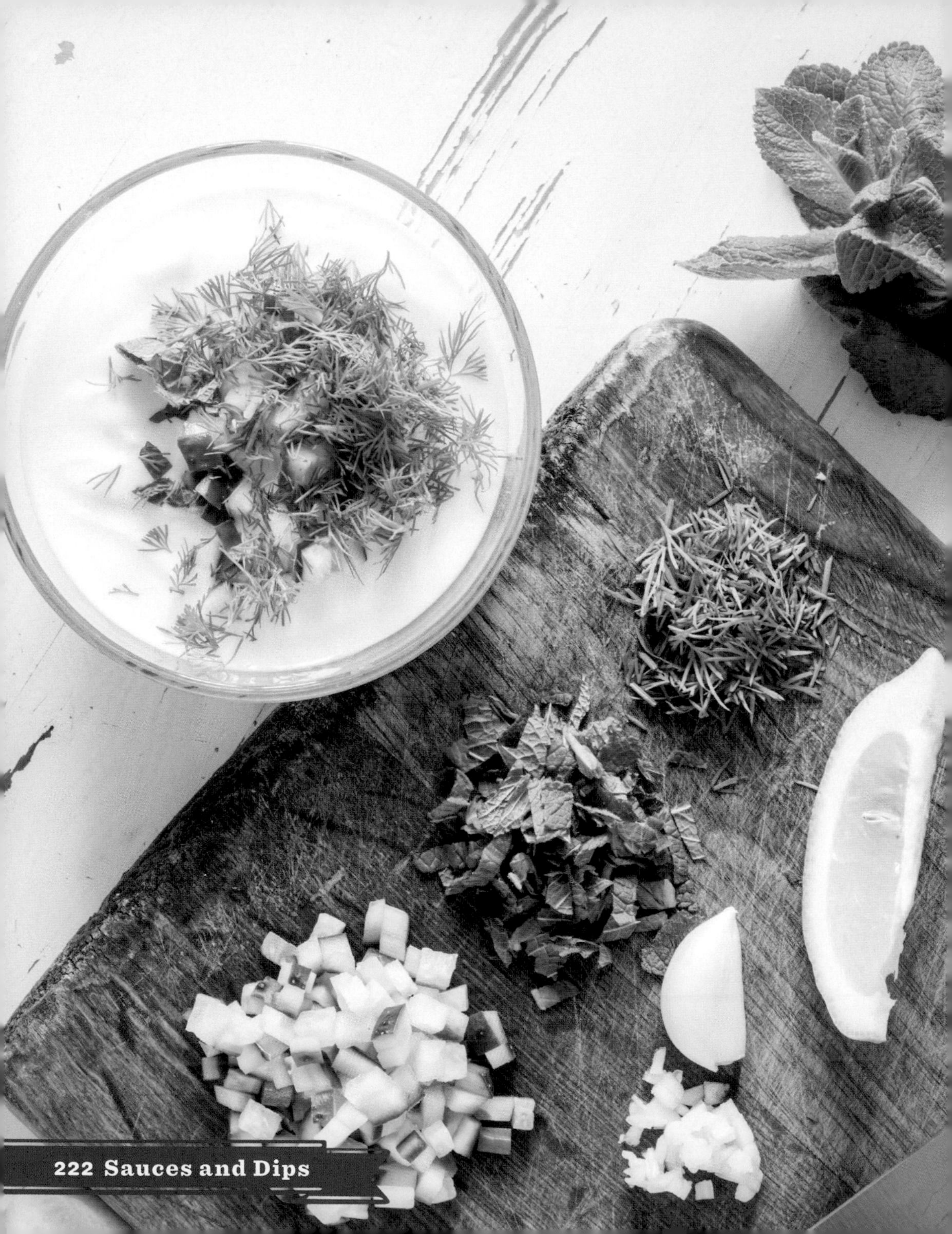

Whisk ingredients in a small bowl until the mixture has emulsified.

1 cup plain Greek yogurt

⅓ hothouse cucumber, diced

1 clove garlic, minced

1 teaspoon salt

1 teaspoon black pepper, freshly ground

3 tablespoons olive oil

1 tablespoon red wine vinegar

1 tablespoon lemon juice, freshly squeezed

1 teaspoon dill (optional)

1 teaspoon mint

Dill Aioli

Everybody loves an aioli, but don't fret if dill isn't your favorite ingredient. I've offered several alternatives below!

INGREDIENTS:

10 sprigs dill, finely chopped

10 sprigs parsley, finely chopped

¼ cup lemon juice, freshly squeezed

1 garlic clove, minced

¾ cup olive oil

1 teaspoon salt

Set the oil aside and blend the other ingredients, slowly drizzling in the olive oil until blended evenly.

REPLACE DILL WITH ANY OF THESE ALTERNATIVES (ALL MEASUREMENTS EQUAL):

- THYME
- ROSEMARY
- CILANTRO
- BASIL
- TARRAGON
- SAGE

Almond Dipping Sauce

Whether using this sauce to dip chicken strips or spring rolls, you might want to plan ahead and just double the ingredients.

INGREDIENTS:

½ cup smooth almond butter

1½ cups coconut milk

1 tablespoon lime juice

1 tablespoon fish sauce

½ teaspoon black pepper, freshly ground

½ teaspoon salt

Cook over medium heat for 3–4 minutes, stirring occasionally. When properly fragrant, remove from heat and serve.

Citrus Salsa

ACTIVE TIME: 10 MINUTES • TOTAL TIME: 10 MINUTES • SERVING SIZE: 1½ CUP

Here's a well-balanced salsa, made to top any taco or be added to any chip!

Whisk ingredients in a small bowl until the mixture has emulsified.

INGREDIENTS:

1 cup pineapple, diced

¼ cucumber, diced

¼ cup mango, diced

1 small shallot, minced

2 tablespoons red pepper, diced

1 tablespoon cilantro

2 tablespoons lime juice, freshly squeezed

2–3 dashes hot sauce

1 teaspoon black pepper, freshly ground

1 teaspoon salt

Tomatillo Salsa

Tomatillo Salsa isn't just for tortilla chips—try it over any beef, pork or chicken dish to add a burst of flavor. Be sure to adjust the jalapeno measurement to your preferred level of spiciness.

INGREDIENTS:

8 tomatillos, halved

1 shallot, thinly sliced

2 cloves garlic

2 teaspoons coriander seeds

1 teaspoon cumin seeds

1 tablespoon salt

1 teaspoon black pepper, freshly ground

2 tablespoons olive oil

1 teaspoon honey

2 cups cilantro leaves

1 jalapeno, chopped

¼ cup water

½ cup lime juice, freshly squeezed

1 Preheat the oven to 400 degrees Fahrenheit. Toss the tomatillos, onion, garlic, jalapeño, coriander, cumin, salt, pepper and oil in a bowl, and then add to a baking sheet.

2 Bake for 20–25 minutes or until vegetables begin to char. Toss once or twice through the cooking time.

3 Once cooled, transfer everything to a blender and blend until smooth. Add lime juice and extra pepper, to taste.

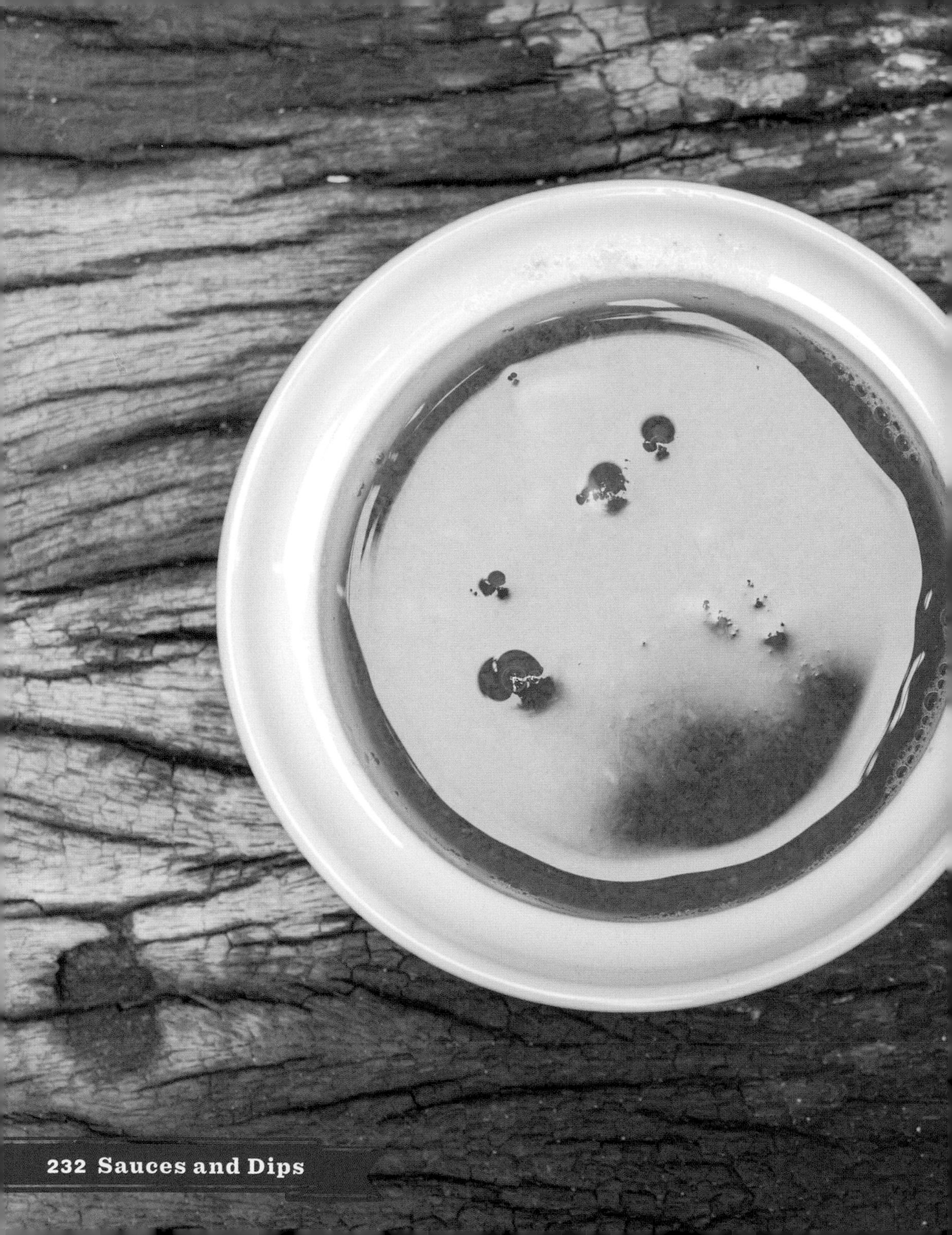

Tamarind Sauce

ACTIVE TIME: 5 MINUTES • TOTAL TIME: 5 MINUTES • SERVING SIZE: 1 CUP

I was first introduced to tamarind while eating Indian food—it's the sweet and savory dipping sauce often served alongside samosas. In dressing form, it works over chicken or a salad of dark bitter greens.

Whisk the ingredients in a small bowl until the mixture has emulsified.

INGREDIENTS:

½ cup olive oil

½ cup balsamic vinegar

1 tablespoon Dijon mustard

1 tablespoon tamarind paste

1 pinch salt

1 pinch brown sugar

Sweet and Tangy Tamarind Sauce

ACTIVE TIME: 5 MINUTES • TOTAL TIME: 5 MINUTES • SERVING SIZE: ¾ CUP

This makes a wonderful dipping sauce for any Asian-inspired appetizer, but I suspect you'll find other uses for it after you first taste!

INGREDIENTS:

½ cup olive oil

1½ tablespoons tamarind paste

1 lime, juiced

1 tablespoon fish sauce

1½ tablespoons honey

Whisk the ingredients in a small bowl until the mixture has emulsified.

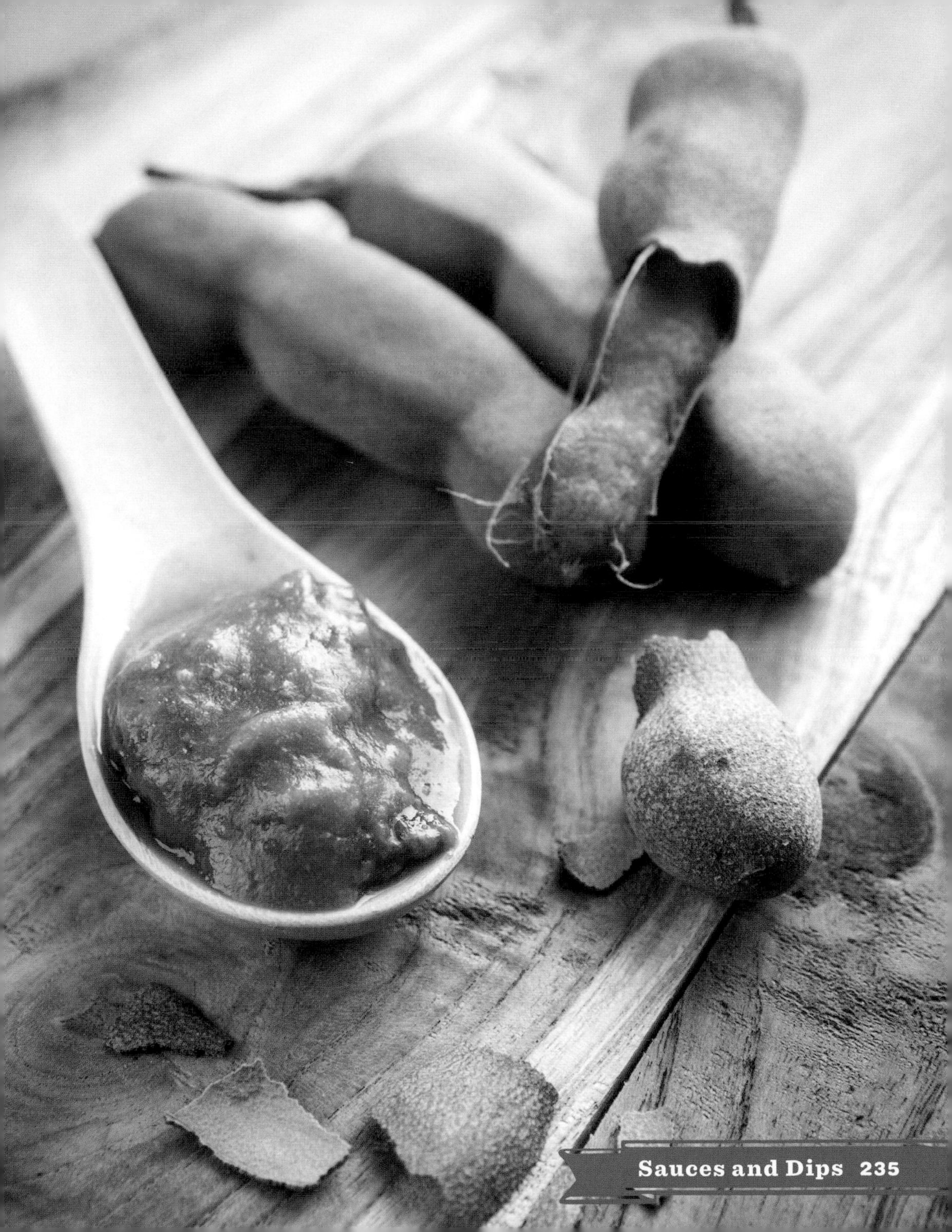

Peanut Tamarind Sauce

ACTIVE TIME: 5 MINUTES • TOTAL TIME: 5 MINUTES • SERVING SIZE: 1 CUP

Just like the sweet and tangy stuff, this tamarind dressing makes a terrific dipping sauce. It's amazing how well peanuts pair with just about anything!

Blend all of the ingredients until the mixture is smooth.

INGREDIENTS:

1 cup low-sodium chicken stock

½ cup crunchy peanut butter

2 tablespoons tamarind pulp

1 small red chili pepper, finely chopped

1½ teaspoons fresh ginger, minced

Cocktail Sauce

For your holiday shrimp!

INGREDIENTS:

1 cup ketchup

1 tablespoon Sriracha sauce

1 tablespoon chili garlic sauce

2 tablespoons lime juice

2 tablespoons ginger, grated

1 teaspoon soy sauce

Whisk ingredients in a small bowl until they've mixed evenly.

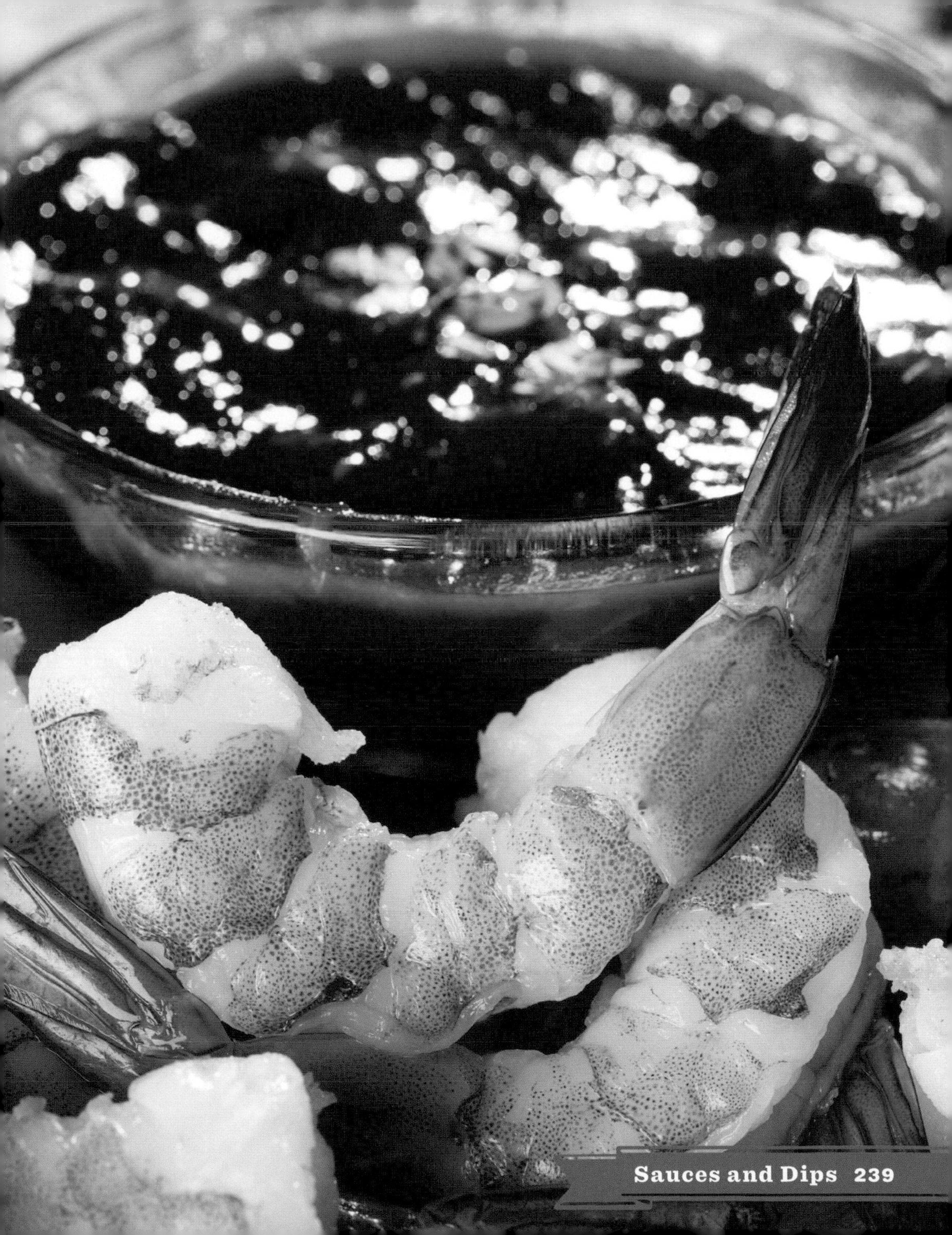

Classic Mignonette

Shellfish-lovers everywhere, it's time to flaunt your bona fides! Classic mignonettes are so easy to make, yet you rarely them homemade. Try this out with your favorite east or west coast oyster!

INGREDIENTS:

½ cup Red wine vinegar

1 shallot, finely chopped

1 teaspoon salt

1 teaspoon black pepper

Stir the ingredients in a bowl until they've mixed evenly.

THERE ARE SO MANY VARIATIONS ON THE CLASSIC MIGNONETTE, IT'S IMPOSSIBLE TO NAME THEM ALL. HERE ARE SOME OF THE MANY ALTERNATIVES YOU MIGHT WANT TO TRY.

- **PEPPERCORN MIGNONETTE:** Add ½ teaspoon of crushed pink peppercorns.

- **RED CHILI MIGNONETTE:** Add ½ teaspoon of red chili flakes

- **CILANTRO MIGNONETTE:** Add 2 teaspoons of finely chopped cilantro.

- **SAKE MIGNONETTE:** Replace the red wine vinegar with ⅓ cup of rice wine vinegar and ¼ cup of boiled sake.

- **CHAMPAGNE VINEGAR MIGNONETTE:** Replace red wine vinegar with ½ cup champagne vinegar

- **WHITE BALSAMIC AND PARSLEY MIGNONETTE:** Replace red wine vinegar with ½ cup white balsamic vinegar.

  Add 2 teaspoon fresh Italian parsley, minced.

- **SPARKLING ROSE MIGNONETTE:** Add ¼ cup sparkling rosé wine to classic mignonette recipe

The Sweet Stuff

Never underestimate a dessert dressing! The first time I tasted a fruit salad with dressing it changed my opinion of fruit salad entirely. And sure, fruit salad is a staple at any summer barbeque—but it can easily be adjusted to the current season as long as you buy (or pick!) in-season produce. Hints of citrus, liquor and mint can bring the fruit together and create an entirely new flavor profile. On top of that, many of these sweet dressings taste great on a vegetable-based salad as well!

But enough about the healthy stuff. You're wondering about dessert. So before you ask: *Of course* these recipes complement cake, ice cream, pie and any other dessert you have in mind, and *of course* you should pour this stuff all over your favorite sweet treat.

Bacon-Peach-Bourbon Dressing

ACTIVE TIME: 10 MINUTES • TOTAL TIME: 10 MINUTES • SERVING SIZE: ¾ CUP

Bacon, peaches and bourbon all in one dressing? Prepare for a true crowd pleaser that's sure to kill at any holiday party.

Whisk the ingredients in a small bowl until the mixture has emulsified.

INGREDIENTS:

¼ cup cooked bacon, diced

½ peach, diced

2 tablespoons Bourbon

¼ cup red wine vinegar

1 teaspoon honey

1 teaspoon Dijon mustard

½ cup extra virgin olive oil

Maple Bourbon Dressing

ACTIVE TIME: 15 MINUTES • TOTAL TIME: 15 MINUTES • SERVING SIZE: ¾ CUP

If you can, always try to use pure maple syrup when cooking—no imitation can compare to the woodsy caramelized sweetness of the real thing. Top your dish (salad or dessert—either work) with some cooked bacon and you'll have a real winner.

INGREDIENTS:

1 cup bourbon, reduced over medium heat to ⅓ cup

¼ cup maple syrup

¼ cup apple cider vinegar

1 small shallot, finely chopped

½ teaspoon fresh thyme, finely chopped

1 teaspoon salt

3 tablespoons grape seed or vegetable oil

1 First reduce your bourbon over medium heat in a small saucepan. When it reduces to ⅓ cup, remove from heat and let cool.

2 Whisk the ingredients in a small bowl until the mixture has emulsified.

Rum Dressing

ACTIVE TIME: 5 MINUTES • TOTAL TIME: 25 MINUTES • SERVING SIZE: $1/3$ CUP

This reads like a cocktail, and for good reason; rum and bitters add a fun, boozy kick to your next fruit salad.

Whisk all the ingredients (including your excess orange juice) in a bowl until evenly mixed.

INGREDIENTS:

3 tablespoons honey

3 tablespoons dark rum

dash or Angostura bitters

cup peeled oranges juice

Fruit Salad Dressing

ACTIVE TIME: 5 MINUTES • TOTAL TIME: 5 MINUTES • SERVING SIZE: ½ CUP

Here's a go-to fruit salad dressing that's perfect for any season.

INGREDIENTS:

1 tablespoon honey

½ cup fresh mint, torn

½ cup apple cider

Blend all of the ingredients until the mixture is smooth.

DEPENDING ON YOUR FLAVOR PREFERENCES, YOU MIGHT WANT TO GET CREATIVE WITH THIS EASY TEMPLATE! HERE ARE SOME OF MY FAVORITE ALTERNATIVES:

- REPLACE THE HONEY WITH PURE MAPLE SYRUP.

- ADD 1 TABLESPOON OF SPICED RUM

- ADD 1 TABLESPOON OF POMMEAU (FRENCH APPLE LIQUEUR)

Classic Crème Anglaise

ACTIVE TIME: 20 MINUTES • TOTAL TIME: 20 MINUTES • SERVING SIZE: 1 ½ CUP

Pour this over your favorite fruit, cake or ice cream to make dessert that much more special.

INGREDIENTS:

1 cup whole milk

1 cup heavy cream

¼ cup sugar

1 vanilla bean, scraped

4 large egg yolks

2 tablespoons spiced rum

1 Combine milk, cream and rum in a medium saucepan, scraping in the seeds from vanilla bean and then adding the bean. Bring the mixture to simmer and remove from heat.

2 Before your milk mixture cools completely, whisk egg yolks and sugar in medium bowl. Gradually whisk hot milk mixture into yolk mixture and return to saucepan.

3 Stir over low heat until your mixture thickens. This should take about 5 minutes—be careful not to boil. Strain sauce into bowl, cover and chill until serving.

THERE ARE TONS OF FUN WAYS TO CUSTOMIZE YOUR CRÈME ANGLAISE TO BETTER PAIR WITH YOUR DESSERT. HERE ARE A FEW CLASSICS! FOR ALL OF THESE RECIPES, SIMPLY REPLACE ALL NEW INGREDIENTS TO THE FIRST STEP, AND REPLACE THE EGG AND SUGAR MEASUREMENTS.

LIGHT VANILLA CRÈME ANGLAISE

 2 cups low-fat milk
 ¼ cup sugar
 4 large egg yolks
 1 ½ teaspoons vanilla extract

BLOOD ORANGE CRÈME ANGLAISE (serving size: ⅔ cup)

 ¾ cup heavy cream
 1 teaspoon blood orange zest, finely grated
 ⅓ cup sugar
 ¼ cup freshly squeezed blood orange juice
 3 large egg yolks

STEEPED CINNAMON CRÈME ANGLAISE

 2 cups whole milk
 ⅓ cup sugar
 1 teaspoon cinnamon
 ½ teaspoon fresh nutmeg
 4 large egg yolks

Warm Lychee Dressing

ACTIVE TIME: 25 MINUTES • TOTAL TIME: 25 MINUTES • SERVING SIZE: ⅓ CUP

When I say Grand Marnier, I don't mean the really expensive bottle! Still, use any orange liqueur you can find. This dressing is a nice option for dessert on a cold winter's night.

INGREDIENTS:

2 tablespoons unsalted butter

2 tablespoons dark brown sugar, packed

¼ teaspoon fresh ginger

2 tablespoons Grand Marnier

1 cup of fresh or canned lychees, diced

Cook all the ingredients over medium-low heat until sugar dissolves, stirring occasionally. This should take about 4–6 minutes. Remove from heat and serve immediately.

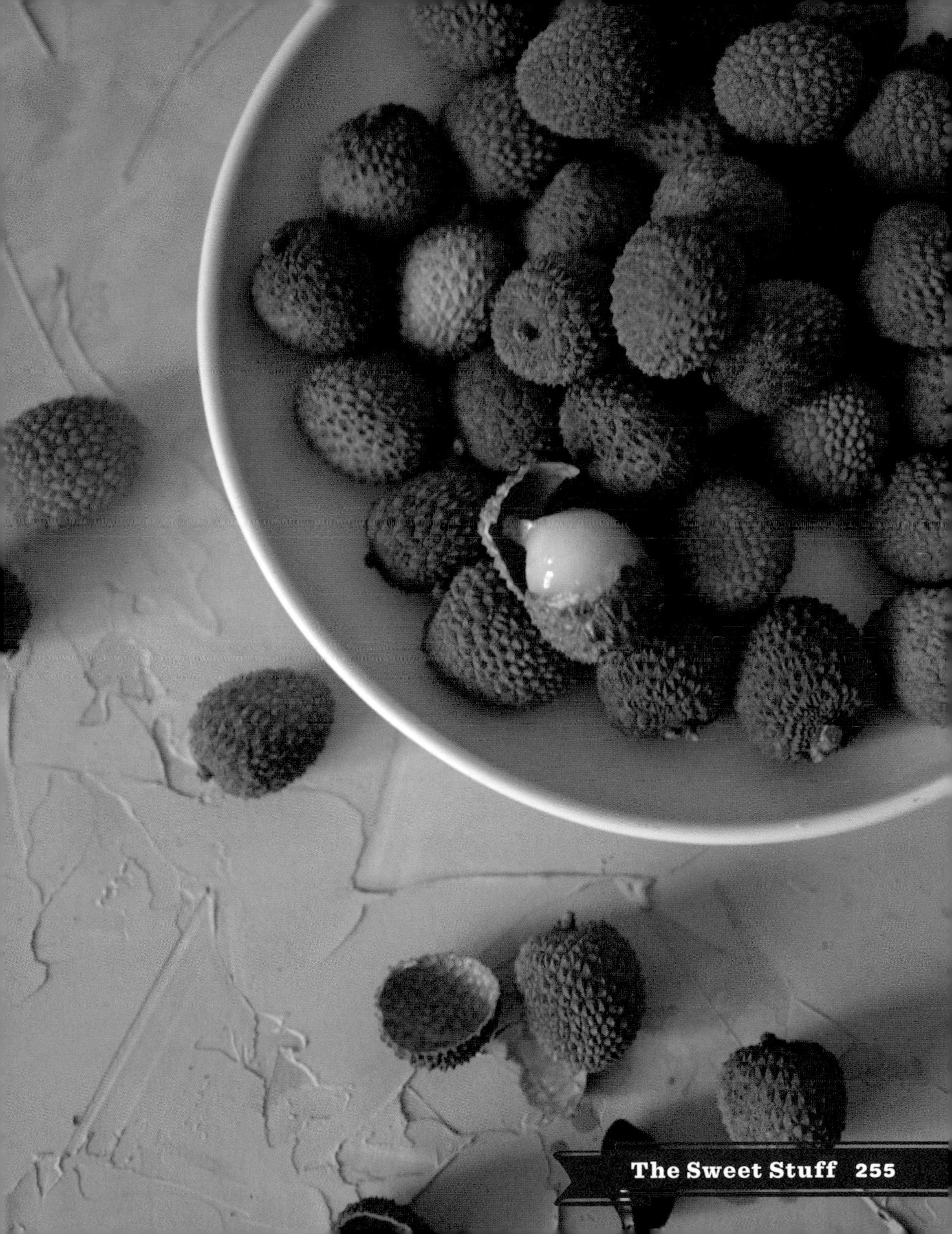

Oil Infusions

A simple olive oil infusion will turn up the flavor volume on any meal. It's so easy to do, and improves anything from a light vinaigrette to a slice of pizza. I like to use different infusions week to week to shake up the basic vinaigrettes I often reuse. These are also perfect gifts for any birthday or holiday. Mix and match flavor combinations to find your favorite new infusion!

Over medium heat, add any of the following ingredients to 1 cup of olive oil:

- 10 sprigs thyme
- 10 sprigs rosemary
- 10 sprigs tarragon
- 1 tablespoon red chili flakes
- 3 cloves garlic, crushed
- 10 sprigs of oregano
- 10 sprigs of lavender

- 1 tablespoon of herbs de Provence
- 2 Thai chilis, diced
- 10 leaves of sage
- 3 dried Bay leaves
- Zest of one lemon
- 2 teaspoons cracked fennel seeds

Index

ACKNOWLEDGMENTS

Writing this cookbook was something I did not believe I had the ability to do. This was a wonderful experience and an exciting challenge, and I hope it's useful to every cook out there. I want to thank my family for their loving support and creativity; my friends for believing I could complete this task; my editor, Patrick Scafidi, for providing the necessary guidance for success; my friend John Whalen III for the initial idea to create this extensive reference; Alicia Freile for such lovely design work; and all the cooking shows I grew up watching and cookbooks I grew up reading for their endless inspiration.

ABOUT THE AUTHOR

Mamie Fennimore is a Philadelphia native currently living and working in Manhattan's Upper East Side as a wineseller. A certified sommelier and former cheesemonger for two of NYC's most reputable cheese companies, she loves to share her knowledge through teaching wine and cheese pairing courses. Her passion for food and wine started at a young age and truly solidified after her time living in the south of France. It was the French lifestyle that inspired her to share the importance of quality dressings and sauces for a meal to bring loved ones to table.

ABOUT CIDER MILL PRESS BOOK PUBLISHERS

Good ideas ripen with time. From seed to harvest, Cider Mill Press brings fine reading, information, and entertainment together between the covers of its creatively crafted books. Our Cider Mill bears fruit twice a year, publishing a new crop of titles each spring and fall.

501 Nelson Place
Nashville, Tennessee 37214

cidermillpress.com